Talking Race
in the Classroom

Talking Race
in the Classroom

Jane Bolgatz

TEACHERS COLLEGE PRESS

Teachers College, Columbia University
New York and London

Published by Teachers College Press, 1234 Amsterdam Avenue, New York, NY 10027

Library of Congress Cataloging-in-Publication Data

Bolgatz, Jane.
    Talking race in the classroom / Jane Bolgatz.
        p. cm.
    Includes bibliographic references and index.
    ISBN 0-8077-4548-0 (cloth: alk paper)—ISBN 0-8077-4547-2 (pbk: alk. paper)
        1. Multicultural education—United States. 2. Racism—Study and teaching—United States. 3. Race relations—Study and teaching—United States. I. Title.

LC 1099.3.B65 2005
370.117—dc22

2004058088

ISBN 0-8077-4547-2 (paper)
ISBN 0-8077-4548-0 (cloth)

My sense is that the American character lives not in one place or the other, but in the gaps between the places, and in our struggle to be together in our differences. It lives not in what has been fully articulated, but in what is in the process of being articulated, not in the smooth-sounding words, but in the very moment that the smooth-sounding words fail us. It is alive right now. We might not like what we see, but in order to change it, we have to see it.

—Anna Deavere Smith, *Fires in the Mirror*

Contents

Acknowledgments

When I began teaching, I wanted to discuss race and racism with my students, but I had little notion of how to do so. In my second year of teaching, I joined the Women Against Racism Committee, a community group in Iowa City, Iowa, that met weekly to discuss issues of race and power. Every Monday, members of the group confronted each other with troubling personal and political questions. We held each other accountable for our prejudices and ignorance. I came to understand Audre Lorde's contention, "It is not our differences that divide us. It is our inability to recognize, accept and celebrate those differences." Even more powerfully, I learned that engaging questions of difference and power often involves tempestuous emotional exchanges, and I learned that I could speak despite my fears. Thank you to committee members Rusty Barcelo, Janet Kaufman, Ju-Pong Lin, Robin Melavalin, Papusa Molina, and Cherry Muhanji for many fervent and demanding discussions.

I would also like to thank the many other people who have contributed to the writing of this book. Bruce Fehn and Cynthia Lewis helped give this research its fundamental shape and direction, and they have continued to extend unwavering support. Ira Baumgarten, Fran Blumberg, Todd Davis, Thaly Germain, Lois Holzman, Soyoung Lee, and Wendy Schwartz gave tremendously helpful feedback to various drafts of the book. Alex Sela and numerous teachers at Fordham University shared insightful stories and dilemmas.

A special thank-you to Jodi Kuhljuergen, who helped me walk the walk; to my mom, Jean Bolgatz, who for hours whittled, questioned, and brainstormed with me; and to Carrie Lobman, who encouraged and guided me with great friendship and joy.

Finally, I want to acknowledge and thank "Lewis," "Ann," and their wonderful students, the sine qua non of this work. They tackled controversy and generously took time to reflect on the process. I hope that these chapters capture and reflect how much they inspired me.

The names and identifying details of all schools, teachers, and students discussed in this book have been changed.

1

Racial Literacy: Talking Even When "the Smooth-Sounding Words Fail Us"

One day in the large comprehensive high school where I taught, June Robinson, a student in my Global Studies class, told me about what had happened earlier that day in her English class. Mr. Taylor and his tenth graders were reading Mark Twain's *The Adventures of Huckleberry Finn*. Brian, a tall boy with spiky brown hair, was reading aloud when the word *nigger* appeared in the text. Brian paused and then looked up at Mr. Taylor. Mr. Taylor glanced at June, the only African American in the class, and then told Brian not to say "the *n*-word." June wondered why Mr. Taylor wouldn't say the word *nigger*.

Classroom conversations about race and racism can be difficult. Often teachers and students—sometimes apologetically, sometimes angrily, but mostly unselfconsciously—avoid the topics altogether. When they do take place, conversations frequently remain superficial or simplistic. Yet if we hope to address the problems that arise as a result of what playwright Anna Deavere Smith (1993) calls "our struggle to be together in our differences" (p. xii), we need to be able to talk meaningfully about race and racism. Just as students need to be literate in traditional ways—able to read, write, and compute—they also need to be what I call racially literate: able to talk with people in order to understand and address racially loaded controversies. Scholar E. D. Hirsch (1987) called for students to develop "cultural literacy" so that they might individually thrive in the world as it is. I call for teachers and students to develop racial literacy so that we might collectively improve our civic society.

Racial literacy is a set of social competencies. Being racially literate means being able to interact with others to challenge undemocratic practices. Racially literate students are willing to break the taboos of

1

talking about race. They can hear and appreciate diverse and unfamiliar experiences. They are genuine about their feelings. They recognize that they have much to learn, and they know how to ask questions. Cultivating racial literacy takes courage. Courage, as Winston Churchill exhorted, "is what it takes to stand up and speak. Courage is also what it takes to sit down and listen."

Racial literacy is not simply a matter of speaking and listening, however. One must view racial issues through a critical lens that attends to current and institutional aspects of racism. Racially literate students understand that various forms of racism have developed historically and that they can contest these practices. I echo religion and African American studies professor Cornel West (1993b), who entreats us to develop civic-minded competence:

> We need leaders—neither saints nor sparkling television personalities—who can situate themselves within a larger historical narrative of this country and our world, who can grasp the complex dynamics of our peoplehood and imagine a future grounded in the best of our past, yet who are attuned to the frightening obstacles that now perplex us (p. 7).

We develop racial literacy—our own and our students'—socially. That is, we learn to talk about race and racism by talking about race and racism. Information and theories that we glean from history, sociology, science, and the popular media are valuable components of understanding racial issues. Becoming racially literate, however, also involves learning how to engage in talk—even when that talk is difficult or awkward. Fortunately and perhaps surprisingly, we foster our racial literacy precisely in those moments when we bump into disagreement and even antagonism. As you will see from the conversations I describe in this book, we can find opportunities to grow and learn when we meet what seems like the most resistance.

CONVERSATIONS CAN BE DIFFICULT

In the discussion of *Huckleberry Finn* above, Mr. Taylor sidestepped talking about race and racism. Teachers, however, are not the only ones who steer away from conversations about race. Law professor Patricia Williams (1997b) described some high school students' avoidance in a Street Law class that was run by law students in a New York City public high school:

[The law students] asked the class of twelfth-graders to break up into small groups and envision that they had to send an expedition of people to populate a new planet. They were to describe the six new architects of the brand-new world, giving their race or ethnicity and their professions. In every group, Hispanics, if they were included, were car mechanics ("They're good at stripping cars" was the explanation some students gave); Asians were included in every group and were always scientists ("They're smart"); whites (including ethnics such as "French," "Italian," "Russian," as well as just "white") had the greatest numerical presence and variety of profession. No blacks were included in the new world (the one student who listed a Nigerian doctor thought Nigeria was in Asia). The kicker is that this school was 53 percent black and 45 percent Hispanic.... Moreover, when the law students attempted to discuss the significance of such impressive skewing, the students...uniformly protested that race had nothing to do with it, and why did the law students (who, by the way, were white) have to "racialize" everything? (pp. 156-157)

In this example, the students perceived the teachers as inappropriately raising questions about race. The teachers, on the other hand, wondered why students would not address what they, the teachers, saw as glaring racial issues.

In other classes, conversations about race upset both students and teachers, who respond by avoiding the topic. Rick Fuentes, a teacher of Spanish in rural upstate New York, described such an incident to me. He was trying to get his students to distinguish between race and culture. The students were uneasy when he told them that race did not really exist.

"Of course races exist," they argued. "There are Black people and White people."

"But," Mr. Fuentes challenged, "there are Black-White people and White-Black people." Indeed, he suggested, "all such classifications are racist, and insisting on race is racist."

This agitated students even more. One student went home and described the conversation to her father, who visited the class a few days later. The confrontation caused quite a stir. The girl and her father went to the principal to complain. The students did not want to revisit the topic. They saw the discussion as a mistake, Fuentes explained, "a trespass that's best not to talk about."

Unlike Mr. Taylor, who simply avoided the word *nigger*, Mr. Fuentes had jumped head first into a conversation about what he thought race meant. However, he did not feel that he had an appropriate strategy to talk with students. Now, rather than critically analyzing concepts such as race and culture, Mr. Fuentes focuses on celebrating ethnicities. His classes study music, cuisine, and dress. Still, Mr. Fuentes wonders how he might talk to students about complex notions of race and racism.

Classrooms are not the only places where students and teachers talk about—and don't talk about—race. Students make inquisitive and incendiary comments in hallways, in cafeterias, and on playing fields. No matter what the setting, students and teachers need racial literacy: the theoretical framework, vocabulary, strategies, and chutzpah that will enable them to engage in conversations about race and racism. Without it, they back away when discussions get uncomfortable.

WHY DO WE HAVE TO TALK ABOUT RACE AND RACISM?

Why, one might ask, should we talk about race at all? Did the law students in the Street Law class really need to have the students declare the race of their new-world architects? Doesn't the question itself accentuate the very differences that are not supposed to matter? And if students repeat the word *nigger*, don't we perpetuate the racism we are supposed to overcome? Martin Luther King Jr. himself said that he hoped his children would not be judged "by the color of their skin but by the content of their character."

Teachers do not want to engage questions of race or racism for many reasons: It is a waste of time, divisive, counterproductive, or rude. While these objections have some basis, I believe the reasons to talk about race and racism outweigh the arguments against doing so. Moreover, we have a particular responsibility to raise these issues with our students. Talking about race and racism in schools is a uniquely meaningful activity for four reasons:

- School is a place where students learn to live democratically.
- We have a moral imperative to teach students about social responsibility.
- Race and racism are critical aspects of the school curriculum.
- Talking about race and racism helps students understand their worlds.

Protecting Democracy

The United States, to borrow a phrase from Lewis, one of the teachers featured in this book, is an ongoing experiment in democracy. A fundamental belief spelled out in the Declaration of Independence and echoed clearly throughout American history—including in King's "I Have a Dream" speech—is that all people are created equal. For the experiment to succeed, we need to guard and nurture this ideal of equality. As West (1993b) explains, "enforced racial hierarchy dooms us as a nation to collective paranoia and hysteria—the unmaking of any democratic order" (p. 4). We cannot afford merely to pay lip service to teaching tolerance or celebrating diversity.

If we agree that democracy is worth protecting and that racism subverts it, then our schools must prepare citizens who can imagine and create ways to change the discriminatory conditions that exist. To do this, we must teach students to recognize inequity. As educational philosopher Maxine Greene (1998) observed:

> It cannot be taken for granted that everyone will notice instances of injustice nor recognize it for what it is. . . . There is the matter of knowing enough (and feeling enough) to argue the cause of justice and persuade others of the importance of moving beyond self-interest to a consideration of their responsibility as members, as citizens. (p. xxx)

To dismantle racism in its myriad forms, students need to know about the history of race relations. They need to know how inequitable politics, economics, and social practices continue to affect the way we live today.

Yet some educators oppose examining race explicitly, arguing that understanding and appreciating the nation's "shared culture" is paramount and that examining differences detracts from establishing effective communities. Historian Arthur Schlesinger (1992), in *The Disuniting of America*, warned about the dangers of paying too much attention to ethnicity and not enough attention to the commonalities of being American. Attention to ethnicity, he argued, distracts people from "joining with the majority in common endeavor" (p. 112). Schlesinger advocated viewing people as individuals, not members of groups or ethnic enclaves.

The "common endeavor" of democracy in the United States, however, has been and still is oppressive to groups, sometimes violently. In struggles to control resources and gain status, American Indians have been forced off their land, Blacks enslaved, Chicanos disenfranchised, and Asians imprisoned and barred from immigrating (Almaguer, 1994; Freehling, 1994; Lepore, 1998; Takaki, 1993). Our history shows that it is impossible to achieve universalism in this country without dealing with racial differences.

Moreover, the idea of a shared, Eurocentric American culture is a myth. While Western European ideas undergird many of our political values, our heritage is composed of a great deal more than these ideas. Peoples from around the world have contributed to and shaped American life and culture. When we respect and value these players and their viewpoints, we reflect the ideal of pluralism on which our country is based. When distinct ethnic, religious, or cultural groups that coexist in the nation assert themselves, they do not fragment the country. They allow our democracy to grow and change.

Indeed, individuals and groups have gained some forms of justice precisely because they have done what Schlesinger so much decries: identified and stood up for themselves as members of oppressed groups. Referring specifically to Blacks fighting for integration in the Montgomery bus boycott in 1955, Martin Luther King Jr. remarked, "when the history books are written in the future, somebody will have to say, 'There lived a race of *black* people, fleecy locks and black complexion, a people who had the moral courage to stand up for their rights. And thereby injected a new meaning into the veins of history and of civilization'"(King, 1955/2001, p.12, emphasis in original). King used identity politics to demand justice that, in the end, benefited everyone.

Young people hold the promise of the future of democracy. That future is in danger if students do not believe in equity. Latino and Black fifth graders I work with in New York City insult each other with names like "dirty Mexican" and "black African." Some think that being American means having blond hair and blue eyes. The students' teasing and their reasoning imply that they and their peers—having neither blond hair nor blue eyes—are not American. I am troubled that these students think they only deserve or will only ever achieve second-class status. When students, no matter what their race, assume that being American means having a certain skin color or class status, they jeopardize the democratic system. For these reasons, we need to look at the ways individuals are treated based on their perceived group membership.

On a daily basis, democracy depends on citizens who can learn from and live with people who have values, experiences and opinions different from their own. If we claim to be preparing students to live, work, and thrive in the 21st century, race and racism need to be a part of the curriculum.

Moral Imperative

Teachers have to cover a lot of academic content. Students need to understand algebraic functions, the Chinese revolution, and polypeptides. However, as we know from the history of Nazi Germany, where political and military leaders were highly educated, concentrating on book smarts alone does not guarantee a good society. Students must also learn to live morally. Combining academic and moral teaching has been a long-standing imperative since the times of Confucius and Plato, and since the earliest schools in the United States were established. "Though goodness without knowledge is weak and feeble, yet knowledge without goodness is dangerous," wrote John Phillips in the mission statement of the prep school Phillips Exeter Academy in 1782. "Both united form the noblest character, and lay the surest foundation of usefulness to mankind."

Teaching goodness is different from making students feel guilty. Guilt is useful to tell us that something is wrong and that we need to do our best to fix it. Beyond that moment, guilt is a waste of time (Lorde, 1984). None of us chose to be born into a hierarchical society. Still, we can recognize that something is wrong and that it is our responsibility as citizens and human beings to work for change.

Teaching students to have a sense of moral obligation is not the same as advocating noblesse oblige, particularly among White students. Whites are no more noble or knowledgeable than anyone else. However, in many circumstances Whites often wield more power than people of color do. White people can acknowledge and take advantage of their particular positions to bring about change. One of the most important ways to act is to raise the issue of race and ask hard questions. Our students need help learning how to do this.

Critical Aspects of Curriculum

In addition to the moral imperative, race and racism should be included in students' coursework because these topics are part of the academic curriculum. Students deserve accurate information in their courses of study. Race and racism are central aspects of history, literature, and science.

"Race has been a major ideology in American life and culture since the colonial era," writes historian James Anderson (1994, p. 87). Race has also played an enormous role in the histories of slavery, colonialism, and globalization. In addition, the lack of attention to race in ancient societies is significant in its contrast with modern society. Yet standard textbooks do not rigorously address the concept or impact of race in history.

Toni Morrison (1992) describes a similar gap in the study of literature: "In matters of race, silence and evasion have historically ruled" (p. 9). In the study of literature, one cannot ignore race, particularly in American literature. As Morrison argued so persuasively in her book *Playing in the Dark*, Africans and African Americans have been central to the construction of what we think of as American. When examining any literature in this country, therefore, it is vital to look at the role of racialized categories. To ignore race and the use of the word *nigger* in a discussion of *Huckleberry Finn*, for example, is to miss a fundamental component of the novel.

Studying about race also helps students understand the theory and practice of science. Although no longer a legitimate area of study, race science, as it was called during the 19th and 20th centuries, was used to distinguish racial groups. Even recently, social scientists have touted racial differences as being related to factors like intelligence (see, for example, *The Bell Curve* [Herrnstein & Murray, 1996]). Yet scientists do not practice in a vacuum. Their work is always subject to the political and cultural influences of their times. Students need to know that the powerful forces of science have vulnerabilities, particularly when it comes to pronouncements about levels of humanity. As historian John Willinsky (1998) argues, "science education has tended to step around its contribution to the construct of race, leaving the young to find themselves at the mercy of this powerful concept with little idea of how it has taken on such importance" (p. 166-167). Without such understanding, students are left to surmise that race is a natural division and that racism is therefore in some sense inevitable.

Some educators argue that schools need to focus on our Eurocentric culture in order to prepare students to be successful in today's world. E. D. Hirsch (1987), in *Cultural Literacy*, for example, suggests that students who have been marginalized in society will have a chance to compete on an even playing field if, among other things, they are introduced to the terms and ideas they need to know to communicate in the dominant culture. To bring about an egalitarian society requires more than just increasing students' "cultural literacy," however. After all, a dominant culture is so named because of the power it wields. Those who disparage paying attention to race or advocate "colorblindness" generally do little to acknowledge or investigate, much less counter, the larger social, political, and economic forces that maintain and foster inequity among racial and other groups.

Even when we share experiences or references, we do not always share interpretations of events. "It is a fallacy of 'cultural literacy,'" wrote scholar Henry Louis Gates (1995) in the aftermath of the O. J. Simpson trial, "to equate shared narratives with shared meanings" (p. 62). There will be disagreements in conversations about race and racism. Indeed, we should welcome dispute. As political theorist Stephen Bronner points out, neutrality "contests repression as little as it fires the imagination" (1999, p.2). We can grow from debates as long as we deal with them respectfully. Taking risks is healthy for students' intellectual development.

Racism Affects Everyone

Violent clashes around the world (ethnic and racial conflicts in Soweto, Kosovo, Kashmir, and Belfast, to name a few) are clear examples of what can happen when groups within a country do not resolve their differences peacefully. We do not have to look beyond our borders to see racial differentiation sparking hostility. Racially charged violence such as that perpetrated against Rodney King and James Byrd Jr. are two examples.

Wherever we turn, issues of race mutter, sing, and shout for our attention. Indeed, sometimes they explode, and those explosions burn. Beyond violence, racism exacts serious personal, social, economic, and cultural costs. Race correlates strongly with poverty and wealth, as well as access to housing and education. Race affects whether you end up in jail, the way you are treated in a restaurant, and even the price you pay for a car (Bonilla-Silva, 2003). Discrimination shuts out and shuts down members of our society every day (Kozol, 1991). Who knows what contributions of inventors, artists, military leaders, athletes, and entrepreneurs we will never enjoy because of opportunities denied and inspirations quashed?

Individually, we have little control over these violent events and institutional barriers to equity. Yet collectively we can respond. We can choose further devastation, as in the violence and destruction in Los Angeles in 1992. Or we can mitigate the dangers, as in the contemplation, reflection, and dialogue that have occurred since 1998 in Jasper, Texas. We can perpetuate racist practices or we can challenge them. Students need to know their options.

Students are curious about issues of race, but fear and inaccurate information hinder their ability to make sense of what they see and hear. The fifth graders I work with can be baffled by the ways that the people around them judge and categorize people. One girl told a group of students about her friend's father, who said that he did not want any light-skinned people in his house. Around the table, her classmates looked at their hands, pulled up their sleeves, and touched their arms. They wondered aloud why someone would not like people because of the color of their skin. A teacher's job is to help students make sense of the divisions and discrepancies around them.

Talking about race and racism can be messy, awkward, or tense. The impulse to avoid the messiness is based, in part, on the reasoning that talking about race can cause pain. As Morrison (1992) explained, "the habit of ignoring race is understood to be a graceful, even generous, liberal gesture" (pp. 9-10). Ironically, the potential for pain is the very indicator of how meaningful conversations about race and racism are. How can we ignore topics that hold such significance in our students' lives?

In addition, in order to teach students effectively, we have to acknowledge and respect their experiences. If we ignore students' race, we send the message that we do not fully accept who they are. Vivian Paley (1979), the MacArthur Award-winning kindergarten teacher, quotes a parent who said, "My children are black. . . . It's a positive difference, an interesting difference, and a comfortable natural difference. At least it could be so, if you teachers learned to value differences more. *What you value, you talk about*" (p. 131; emphasis added). We need to talk about the identities our children bring to the classroom. Such conversations benefit everyone. Educator Gloria Ladson-Billings (1994) praises teachers who draw on experiences that relate to their students' race and culture and who use interactional styles that resemble their students'. This "culturally relevant teaching," as she calls it, helps students to succeed academically and at the same time feel proud about who they are.

White students often assume that they do not have a race or ethnicity. Many think that Whites always and only have been oppressors when it comes to racism, and so they do not want to talk about race. If we talk about race, however, White students can learn about a complex history that includes Whites who have fought for change. Artists and civil rights activists such as Adrienne Rich, Miles Horton, and Morris Dees provide excellent models of Whites who have been active allies in the fight for racial justice.

Some teachers and administrators posit that talking about race might be useful for people of color but is not a concern for teachers in predominantly White schools (Ladson-Billings, 2003; A. Lewis, 2001; Reddy, 1994). However, thinking that racism should be of interest only to certain groups allows White people to continue participating in a racist society without being aware of how they contribute to the problems or how they could play a role in the solutions.

TALK MATTERS

Talking together is a core activity with which to develop racial literacy. Talk is a powerful tool. It develops our ideas and influences who we are.

Talk is also a form of action. Playwright Bertold Brecht said that art was a hammer with which to shape reality. I believe that talk, like art, does not simply mirror reality; it influences reality. Race and racism do not need to be the centerpiece of a curriculum, but these topics need to be brought up when they are relevant and addressed when they come up, even if our attempts are flawed.

Talk gives shape to our ideas. When we talk, we articulate ideas that have not been completely formed. Psychologist Lev Vygotsky (1986) explained, "Thought is restructured as it is transformed into speech. It is not expressed but completed in the word" (p. 251). Talk helps us "complete" our thoughts. Language enables us to articulate notions we might not have fully seen or understood. Listening and speaking can help us know in new ways. New awareness can lead to new feelings. New emotions, in turn, can lead to new ways of acting.

Talking, however tentative, is also itself a form of action. When we talk with others—particularly those considered different from us—we can explore creative ways to interact.

Moreover, *not* talking is its own form of action. A teacher's silence leaves his or her students' assumptions unexamined. Silence denies us the opportunity to try out and share new ideas, positions, or ways of working together.

CAVEATS

As an aside, it should be noted that race does not float in a vacuum. Indeed, we can only fully understand racism when we understand the connections among various forms of oppression (Bartolome & Macedo, 1997). Racism and classism are particularly connected. Whites, as W. E. B. Du Bois noted, are compensated with a "public and psychological wage" for their race as well as with monetary and material rewards (cited in Roediger, 1999). The intersections of oppressions are powerful and have been reinforced historically. White slave owners, for example, wooed lower-class Whites in the South using racial politics in order to interrupt the working-class bonds that they worried would form between poor White farmers and Black slaves (Roark, 1978).

Foregrounding race oversimplifies the question of how we should talk with students about power and oppression. Nonetheless, I believe focusing on one aspect of oppression can give us a starting point from which we might begin to explore myriad parallel and intersecting questions about equity.

Similarly, focusing on race relations in the United States severely limits the scope of our understanding. Race and racial oppression are global phenomena that have specific implications depending on one's location. Even within the United States, geographies differently affect the meanings and consequences of race. Recognizing its limitations, I focus in this book on the United States because the students in the class I observed were taking a U.S. history class.

WE'RE NOT PREPARED TO TALK ABOUT RACE

There are times when conversations about race and racism are so flawed that they can be harmful (M. Wilson, personal communication, May 28, 1999). Conversations in which individuals or groups are stereotyped or degraded convey misinformation. When the misinformation is not countered, the conversations can hurt students. While I believe that educators need to have courage and take risks, we also have to prepare ourselves for difficult conversations and be sensitive to potential dangers.

Most educators have had little training in how to handle thorny exchanges. How to talk about the word *nigger*, or any other aspect of race or racism, for instance, was never a question on the agenda of district in-service meetings where Mr. Taylor and I taught. Neither is the topic usually handled in teacher education courses. Mary Dilg (1999), a White high school English teacher, described both her lack of preparation and the challenges she faced in discussing texts focusing on race:

> To approach effectively these works of literature, the issues they focus on, and the dynamics they trigger among students requires not only a grounding in the literature of multiple cultures, but a knowledge of history, political science, sociology, anthropology, psychology, group dynamics and conflict management—a breadth and depth of background most of us in my generation lack, even after we have gone through well-respected undergraduate and graduate programs in liberal arts. (p. 7)

Few teachers are taught how to be racially literate, so we do not know how to help our students learn these skills. Not knowing how to handle the controversies, we are unwilling to wander into what we perceive to be dangerous waters.

As a White teacher in predominantly White schools, I often heard students make statements related to race that made me uncomfortable. I remember my awkward silence as students in a World History class negatively described the "exotic" people and "weird" places they would "encounter" in Latin America. We had discussed ethnocentrism, yet students still described as abnormal people whom they perceived as different. The students acted as if their experiences as White, middle-class people living in the United States should be the standard by which to judge others—often disapprovingly. I did not know how to talk with them about these subtle forms of degradation. In later years, when I tried to help students examine their assumptions and misconceptions, explorations of racism often got lost in rapid and sometimes angry exchanges that precluded thoughtful discussion.

THE STUDY OF ONE CLASSROOM

Over the years, I took more risks and became more comfortable and articulate in discussions with students. There were still difficult exchanges, however, and I thought it would be useful to formally study those confounding moments. As a researcher, I decided to go back to the high school where I had taught for 5 years. I asked two former colleagues if I could sit in on their team-taught U. S. History and Language Arts class to study their conversations. They agreed.

I knew that I was not going to find one best way to talk about race or racism. Each classroom is a distinct environment with unique pressures, goals, and circumstances. The class I observed was neither a model to emulate nor a straw man. Rather, it was a place to investigate real conversations. In this book, I reflect on that class in order to illuminate some of the possibilities and pitfalls in addressing issues of race and racism with students. How do students and teachers talk about race and racism? How are conversations initiated, and what helps them develop? These questions guided me in observing Lewis and Ann's class.

Lewis and Ann's Class

Lewis Shirer and Ann Gerard were two hardworking teachers at Central High School, a small public school in Riverville, a predominantly White, midwestern city of about 114,000 whose population was almost 95% Non-Hispanic White, almost 3% Black, 1% Asian, 0.2% American Indian, and 1% Hispanic (U. S. Census Bureau, 1998). Lewis and Ann team-taught a multigrade, interdisciplinary Language Arts and U.S. history class. Among the many goals and responsibilities they had, Ann and Lewis wanted their high school students to think about race and racism. I chose Ann and Lewis's class for three reasons.

- The class was a required course, not an elective about race or oppression. I wanted to observe a cross section of students in the context of a general course rather than students specifically interested in race or racism, or a class devoted to those topics.
- The teachers were interested in issues of race and oppression. I suspected that the topic would come up in discussions.
- I had a great deal of respect for both Lewis and Ann as teachers. I admired their honesty and openness in the classroom. Having taught with them before, I knew firsthand about their willingness to try new things and their caring and high standards for students and education.

Central High School is an alternative school for students who were at risk of dropping out of school entirely. The teachers had a great deal of flexibility in how they adhered to district curricula. While this class was not in a traditional school, it was conventional in the sense that the teachers' goals were to teach language arts and American history, not about race specifically. The conversations—save, perhaps, for some expletives forbidden in other settings—could have taken place in a traditional school classroom.

Research Methodology

I sat in on Lewis and Ann's class for one 12-week term, participating in conversations and tape-recording discussions. When asked how he saw me in the class, one student said I was "like one of those guys with their notebooks in the back of a press conference, just taking down information, not being partial one way or the other. Just getting the information that you need to get down, and if you feel fit, ask[ing] a question now and then." Outside class, I continued this stance. I interviewed the students and teachers about what was happening in the class. I visited students' homes and sat in on teachers' planning sessions and staff meetings. I interacted with the students and teachers as a participant-observer. I would occasionally give feedback or suggestions. Sometimes I would ask questions in class, while much of the time I quietly observed and recorded my observations.

During and after the term, I reflected on the class. I also transcribed the bulk of the class discussions and interviews. Reading and rereading these notes and transcripts, as well as secondary data sources such as the students' class notes, I developed categories of analysis (Strauss, 1987) about when and how students talked about race and racism. As I reached tentative conclusions during and after the term, I would check in with the teachers and students to get feedback about the validity of my perceptions (Merriam, 1988).

Who I am undoubtedly affected students' and teachers' perceptions of me and affected the extent and ways in which they shared their ideas. I was a 33-year-old, middle-class White woman. On the first day of the term, the teachers introduced me as a friend, a former teacher at the school, and a person the students could trust.

Focus on Group Interactions

When I was first searching for ways to understand conversations about race and racism in my own classroom, I came across theories about how people's emotions, ideas, and assumptions about race and racism evolve (particularly useful explanations and examples of racial identity development theory are provided by Carter, 1997; Fine & Weis, 1993; Helms, 1990; Smith, 1998; and Tatum, 1992). I knew, however, that the difficulties I faced in discussing controversial issues such as racial oppression did not exist simply because students somehow had insufficient understanding or inaccurate ideas. Classes are complicated by the ways in which students and teachers together, through complex interpersonal dynamics, pull and push discussions in various directions. Because the ways in which we talk depend as much on the dynamics within the classroom as on individuals' ideas, emotions, and beliefs, this book focuses more on the interactions among teachers and students than on the psychology of individuals.

Talk is always contextualized (Tobin, 2000). What we say and how we talk depends on the situation. I talk differently about an illness, a romantic relationship, or my bank account depending on whether I am talking to my mother or a new coworker. I express myself differently even about the same topic depending on whether I am talking on a public bus or in my living room. What students say in the classroom, therefore, is not the expression of constantly held beliefs. Rather, students make particular statements that reflect their location in a particular social environment.

Group dynamics make classrooms complicated. Groups can inhibit speakers, but talking in groups has its advantages. Students and teachers talking together can "complete" thoughts for one another (Vygotsky, 1986). Thus a group can understand and think in more sophisticated ways than any one person could do individually (Lobman, 2003).

TERMINOLOGY

Language about race is imprecise; words lump people into monolithic groups based on indeterminate notions that are often a mixture of ethnicity, nationality, and geography as well as physical features. Throughout this book, I use concepts that are socially constructed and therefore amorphous and changing. By race, I am not simply talking about the color of one's skin, the shape of one's nose, or the cultural differences associated with various ethnic groups. I am also referring to the systems of privilege and disadvantage connected to what we call race. Chapter 2 addresses the meanings of race and racism in detail.

In deciding how to describe participants, I asked the students and teachers themselves for guidance (see Maggio, 1997; Nieto, 2000). Thus, for example, I use *Asian* or *Korean* to refer to Vic and *Chicano* to refer to Flores, because these students described themselves with those terms. I capitalize *Black* and *White* for similar reasons. First, I asked Lewis, one of the two teachers, what term he used to describe himself. He said, "Black, with a capital B." I asked Ann, the other teacher, the same question. She said she called herself "White." For the sake of consistency, and because I wanted to call attention to the difference between black and white as colors and Black and White as socially constructed racial labels, I decided to capitalize both descriptors. Several of the students referred to themselves or others as White or Black, so unless there was a specific reason for me to do otherwise, I use those terms. I list students' self-designated races in the chart of participants in Appendix A, but I do not use racial markers in the bulk of the description and analysis of the class.

People of color is a particularly imprecise term. It denies the particular histories of vastly different peoples. Having said this, I use this term because it was the one most preferred by the students and teachers in the class. Similarly, *American Indian* is a term used to describe numerous, distinct nations and groups. I use it because it is often used by Native peoples (Rains, 2003).

ORGANIZATION OF THE BOOK

Chapter 2 offers the theoretical grounding for developing racial literacy. I explain race as a social and historical construction and describe various elements of individual and institutional forms of racism. I review the ways in which educational theorists have suggested that teachers help students learn about race and racism.

In contrast to the theoretical focus of Chapter 2, Chapter 3 is a case study of how a class of lively students along with their teachers tackled issues of race and racism in the course of one term. I suspect that readers will identify with some of the teachers' dilemmas or recognize some of the students' voices. The study of this class is the basis for the analysis in the rest of the book.

Chapter 3 shows that while conversations sometimes feel chaotic, students can and do address serious issues related to race and racism. Chapter 4 delineates the ways in which Lewis, Ann, and the students created and extended opportunities for discussions. The teachers put the issues of race and racism on the table. They modeled and encouraged exchanges with personal stories, anecdotes, and questions. Their curricular decisions and initiative encouraged the students to reflect about the meaning and consequences of race and racism.

Chapter 5 describes the ways in which students tacitly defined race and racism. Students sometimes saw race as fixed, and they took stances of colorblindness. They also characterized racism as a thing of the past or as personal or extreme. I describe how teachers can challenge these interpretations so that students expand their repertoire of tools for racial literacy.

Chapter 6 looks at how students responded to their teachers and peers and how those dynamics affected discussions. I explore the reasons that students and teachers sometimes avoided talking about race or racism and what can be done to cultivate conversations, given students' and teachers' assumptions, needs, and inclinations.

Chapter 7 concludes with a discussion of ways for teachers to understand and enhance their own and their students' racial literacy. I also suggest how administrators can cultivate an environment that values racial literacy. Every setting has particular challenges. I believe we can develop students' racial literacy no matter where we are.

CONCLUSION

Schools and communities throughout the United States are very racially segregated. Most of our students, therefore, have little contact with people of different races (Orfield & Lee, 2004). Without forces or experiences intervening to mitigate their ignorance about different races, students can easily perpetuate stereotypes and myths and harden racial divisions. Moreover, no matter how they identify themselves racially, students benefit from understanding how racism affects them and how they participate in racism, even by their silence.

Classroom conversations about race can be awkward or aggressive, leaving us feeling incredulous: "How can students be so racist?" Or mystified: "What did she mean?" Or stymied: "They didn't want to hear a word I said!"

Yet it is possible to transform the skepticism into trust and the silence into dialogue. Racial literacy gives students and teachers an analytical framework and the wherewithal we need when "the smooth-sounding words fail us" (Smith, 1993, p. xii) when we find ourselves getting stuck or angry. Racial literacy allows us to address the stereotyping, jokes, and defensiveness that go on in our classrooms and cafeterias. Our students *can* become more conscious, more critical, and more confident. Racial literacy allows us to create contexts where thoughtful and provocative interactions occur.

Students need to learn to be citizens active in constructing and maintaining a society that accords everyone equal rights. To do so, they need to know how to challenge racism and to believe that they can do so. To educate students to these ends is an enormous challenge and a vital one. Happily for teachers who need a reason to address these issues, race is an integral feature of history, literature, current events, and other topics that students need to study. Debate about race and racism is a worthy intellectual endeavor.

In short, if we are to promote democracy, justice, and academic integrity, and make schooling challenging and relevant for students, we need to figure out compelling and productive ways to include race and racism in our curricula. We need to have conversations with students that allow us to explore how race affects our lives, how we shape definitions of race, how racism worked in the past, how it works today, and how we can act to interrupt racist ideologies and dismantle racist practices.

This book is for teachers who, like Mr. Taylor, have avoided talking about race and racism for any number of reasons. It is also for teachers who, like the law students, Mr. Fuentes, and me, have been perplexed by interactions with students and who are looking for ways to understand and address the silence, antagonism, and confusion that often surround issues of race and racism.

My hope is that developing the tools of racial literacy will help alleviate that tongue-tied frustration we so often feel. I hope teachers and others will use the skills of racial literacy to engage students, colleagues, friends, and strangers. Conversations about race profoundly affect our students' lives, and they have power to influence our society's collective strength. We can help students build their capacity to understand and confront racism in society. Doing so begins in individual classrooms, one conversation at a time.

2

What Is Race? What Is Racism?

It is easy to forget that categories we often take for granted—American Indian, Asian, biracial, Black, Latino, person of color, White, and so on—do not really describe people. Labels have all sorts of connotations, and meanings change over time. Racism is also a chameleon that looks different in different times and locations. Genocide, lynching, and other violent acts, as well as institutionalized discrimination and individual prejudice, are all manifestations of racism. The weapons and wounds of racial bias are sometimes blatant, but they also can be harder to trace. This chapter explains how I view race and racism so we might share a common understanding of these contentious terms. To do so, I look at scientific and sociological definitions of race, and I address how prejudice and discrimination are linked to larger issues of power and oppression.

Theory is like a road map. While it cannot tell us about all the bends or obstacles in the road, it can point us to major routes and destinations. Throughout this chapter, I call on the many historians, sociologists, and civil rights advocates whose theories inform my understanding of what *race* and *racism* mean. In addition, I draw on activists and educational researchers as I invite readers to think in new ways about how to talk with students about the topics.

WHAT IS RACE?

The Science of Race

If race represented a biological reality, we would have no trouble defining what it means to be a member of a certain race, and everyone around the world would hold the same definitions. Instead, people constantly debate who is what (Davis, 1991; Yancey, 2003). While historically people have expressed and reinforced notions that race is natural and that racial differences are inborn, current scholarship disputes race as a scientific concept. DNA research shows that there are likely to be more physical differences between two people of the same "race" than between two people of different "races" (American Anthropological Association, 1998). Scientists actually cannot define the broad racial categories we often relate to attributes such as skin color, facial features, hair color and texture, and other physical aspects of human beings.

Despite the scientific repudiation of race as a viable category, people are still tied to perceptions of race as an aspect of identity. When Rick Fuentes, the Spanish teacher described in Chapter 1, told his class that "there are Black-White people and White-Black people," he was trying to get his students to realize that racial categories are not simple biological entities. As Rick found out, however, people can be strongly attached to considering race as given and fixed.

We describe and classify others according to how we perceive them racially (as well as in terms of our perceived notions of gender, class, nationality, and so on): "that Black guy," "the Asian lady." The ways in which we identify ourselves and are identified by others affect everything from mortgage rates to blind dates. We check off boxes proclaiming our race on college and job applications, on government census forms and contract applications. Hence, although our physical differences may be biologically insignificant, race profoundly affects our lives and life chances.

The Historical and Social Construction of Race

A building does not spring out of the ground naturally. With a great deal of skill and flair, masons, steelworkers, electricians, and many other people work together to build it. When the workers finish, however, you usually cannot see the process of their construction in the final product. The footings, beams, pipes, and insulation are all hidden. Similarly, ideas do not simply spring into existence. Particular social, economic, and political forces shape their meanings. There is a "preliminary mental ordering," explains historian Roger Darnton (1985) "that goes into the common-sense notion of the real world. Common sense itself is a social construction of reality, which varies from culture to culture" (p. 23). Moreover, notions about the way the world is continually evolve. Yet the process of construction remains invisible.

Race is a particularly inchoate and contested idea. We often mistake race as having a commonsense definition instead of being, as sociologists Omi and Winant (1986) call it, a "sociohistorical" concept. Racial categories and meanings have changed through history (Anderson, 1994; Davis, 1991; Willinsky, 1998). In the mid-1800s, for instance, Irish immigrants to the United States were not seen as deserving the privileges accorded to Whites and faced discrimination in jobs and housing. By the 1900s, however, the Irish had begun to develop political and economic power (by, among other means, specifically distinguishing themselves from Blacks) and had lost the stigma attached to their nationality. A century later, people of Irish decent are generally considered White (Ignatiev, 1995; Roediger, 1999; Takaki, 1993).

When we ignore our history, we come to believe that differences across so-called racial groups are tied to biological factors. "Black English," for example, is not the result of inferior intelligence or an unwillingness to learn. Whereas my grandmother, a Jewish immigrant from Eastern Europe, could go to night school to learn English, laws banned Black slaves arriving from Africa from learning to read. Slaves developed a way of speaking English, complete with grammatical rules. Those who see "Black English" as a sign of natural inferiority disregard how laws made by Whites demanded that Blacks develop this language. Indeed, "Black English" is an ingenious response to an unjust system.

Perceptions of race and other aspects of identity depend on social context as well as history. Students in a public school in Cedar Rapids, Iowa, read my curly brown hair and olive white skin differently than the faculty at the University of Iowa do. Students in one public school in New York City read them differently again than do my university colleagues in the same city, or, indeed, students in a different school. Each individual in these settings views me through lenses shaped by his or her experiences. In New York City, many people assume I am Jewish. In Cedar Rapids, where the Jewish population is much smaller, none of my students guessed that I might be Jewish. "Are you Mexican?" they asked. "Indian?" As the child of a Jewish father and a Christian mother, I hadn't considered myself Jewish until I moved from New York City, where those characteristics that signified my "Jewishness" were never noted. Perceptions of race and identity—one's own and others'—are constantly shifting.

Meanings attributed to differences such as race and gender are constructed and reinforced through language. Meanings continually change. The process of constructing ideas is often so subtle that we often don't even notice (Gee, 1994). When we talk, we are influenced by those around us, and we draw on the "voices" that each of us carries from his or her previous experiences (Erickson, 1986; Wertsch, 1991). Together we can create new meanings for racial categories. These meanings include and determine the importance of the categories. Students in the Street Law class in Chapter 1, for instance, described Hispanics as car mechanics because "they're good at stripping cars" and Asians as scientists because "they're smart." In doing so, the students reinforced or added to the meanings of existing racial labels.

While we may be influenced by those around us, meanings are not universal. The ways we use and interpret language vary among people, and there are always power dynamics at work in our interpretations. Some of my students who are Black have argued that Black musicians Run DMC and Puffy (Sean) Combs are icons of power. When I thought of people in power, I immediately thought about the president of the United States, who is White. We each have legitimate arguments that reflect our values and views about the meaning of power. Those underlying values may or may not be clearly articulated or examined, but nonetheless they are reflected in our use and interpretation of language.

There is often tension between race as social construction and race as biology. In writing this book, I was torn between wanting readers to get a vivid picture of the students and teachers, and worrying that using racial markers to describe the individuals would reinforce the notion that you can glean anything about a person from knowing the shade of her skin or the color of his hair. I did not want to bias readers, and so, in the end, I chose to avoid racial descriptors for the bulk of my analysis. However, knowing that race is socially constructed and that one's race does affect one's experiences in the world, I included students' and teachers' self-identifications when they were relevant to a particular point.

Race Is Not a Neutral Category

Race and racial terms are loaded, steeped in histories in which power was, and still is, established and contested. Race does not just mean skin color, but as Toni Morrison (1992) explained, "Race has become metaphorical— a way of referring to and disguising forces, events, classes, and expressions of social decay and economic division far more threatening to the body politic than biological 'race' ever was" (p. 63). Racial labels can be codes to imply that someone is powerful, poor, dangerous, or oppressing.

Labels are insidious in that they hide the ways in which inequities are made to seem natural. Language constructs certain subjects as normal and marginalizes and exoticizes others. A newspaper, for example, notes the race of a presidential candidate only when the candidate is something other than White. Similarly, a radio broadcast reports on suicide bombers and female suicide bombers. There is a National Basketball Association and a Women's National Basketball Association (as opposed to one association with two divisions). The distinctions may appear to be simply a matter of numbers, but the implications are influential. These uses of language subtly condition us to expect or approve of certain people to become president of the United States, carry out a bombing, or play basketball.

People in power, according to poet Gloria Yamato (1990), "are purported to have an innate ability to access economic resources, information, respect, etc., while the oppressed are believed to have a corresponding negative innate ability" (p. 20). How did we come to believe that certain groups of people have "innate abilities" based on their race that others lack? Many historians and sociologists believe that the concept of race was developed as Europeans began to colonize lands in the 15th, 16th, and 17th centuries (Bonilla-Silva, 2003; Fredrickson, 2002). In colonial America, for example, laws referred to Negroes, Whites, and Indians beginning in the 1600s (Takaki, 1993). The process of determining and shifting the meanings of race has not been neutral. Definitions of race have painted Whites as naturally superior. These claims, often combined with views of religious and cultural superiority, were used to justify enslaving Africans, assimilating American Indians, and bestowing land and the fruits of other people's labor to Whites (Willinsky, 1998).

TEACHING ABOUT RACE

When students talk about differences, they often do not seem to recognize their own perceptions as anything but "normal" (Hatcher & Troyna, 1993). Educational theorists suggest that teachers help student examine the histories of racial groups and investigate how we know about these histories.

Heroes and Holidays Are Not Enough

One of the most popular ways teachers begin to broach the topic of race is the "heroes and holidays" approach. For instance, in December, elementary students learn about Kwanza, Ramadan, Hanukkah, and Christmas. In February, they learn the story of Rosa Parks. High school students learn about Blacks in slavery and again during the civil rights movement. They might also read (usually in sidebars) about individuals such as Chief Seattle and Cesar Chavez. The problem with this approach is that it sends inaccurate and disempowering messages. It implies that racial groups exist only at certain times and that the stories of individuals represent whole groups (Anderson, 1994).

Scholars know a great deal about the ways in which individuals and groups have participated in history. Often schoolchildren learn little about that collective power. Students might learn about Martin Luther King Jr. as a hero, for instance, but not understand the great strength in the African American community upon which King drew. When I talked with a class of fourth graders about the treatment of Blacks on buses before the Montgomery bus boycott, for instance, and asked what would happen if similar civil rights violations happened today, one of the most articulate students in the class said, "No one would be able to stop it because Martin Luther King is dead." The student saw King as a savior without realizing that many people helped in the fight for civil rights.

Examine the Construction of Race

Teachers and students need to guard against implying that Whiteness or any other position is or should be a norm or standard by which "others" are judged (Fine, Weis, Powell, & Wong, 1997). To move beyond heroes and holidays, educators suggest that we help students uncover and problematize the often hidden social and historical construction of race (Banks, 1997; Kincheloe & Steinberg, 1998; Nieto, 2000; Sleeter, 1993; Sleeter & McLaren, 1995). Teachers can encourage students not to generalize about racial differences or assume that those purported differences are natural and therefore immutable. We can help students understand that race is a social construction by showing them that race and racial differences have been constructed in particular ways by people over time. Students may be able to debunk the stereotype that Blacks are lazy, for instance, if they learn how that stereotype came to be. Slave masters in the United States, not reckoning that slaves had the wherewithal to act on their own volition, judged as lazy the slaves who worked slowly. The owners did not recognize that their slaves were purposefully slowing down their work as a way to resist the condition of slavery (Genovese, 1974). Students who do not know where the stereotype came from may not know what to do with it other than believe it and, worse yet, reproduce it. They are not likely to challenge the stereotype or recognize it in its various permutations in society (in the myth of the Black welfare queen, for instance).

Students can interrogate the implications of language. They can mold new meanings for words and rethink their own racial identities. Students can only critique what they are able to see. If Whites perceive Whiteness to mean having power over people of other races, for instance, they might blindly walk into that role. We need to help them understand the ways that Whiteness has *evolved* into being a status deserving to have power over others.

Educators Wills and Mehan (1996) warn against teaching "the cultural attributes of specific groups as static and fixed" (p. 6). Too often lessons about racial difference leave students with the impression that there is something wrong with people of color. Rather, students should learn about members of cultural groups as active agents in particular events in history (Levstik & Barton, 2001). Rather than learning only about the cultures of indigenous peoples in pre-colonial times, for example, students could learn about the role of Navajo Marines in World War II as military code-breakers and about the current struggles for land rights among the Oneida and other nations. Jazz musicians in the Harlem Renaissance were not only pioneering Black professionals; they also, and perhaps more importantly, significantly influenced the course of American music.

WHAT IS RACISM?

There is only a thin line between defining *race* and perpetuating racism. As historian James Anderson (1994) explains, "Racists make the claim that particular human populations ('races') create superior civilizations, conquer vast territories, and dominate other human groups (other 'races') because they are intellectually superior—and that differences between 'races' are mainly a result of immutable genetic factors and not of environmental or historical circumstances" (p. 90). Like race, racism is established, shaped, and maintained through everyday social practices, such as representations in the media and the curricula used in schools. If the only thing I learn about great civilizations is about the territories and domination of "the West" and not others, I learn to perpetuate the racist notions Anderson described.

Racism, however, isn't always articulated so blatantly. People can display what education professor Joyce King (1991) calls "dysconscious racism," in which inequity is unquestioned or tolerated because it is seen as part of the way the world simply *is*. Equally pernicious, laws and economic practices implement and perpetuate racism. The phone company, for instance, might redline my predominantly Puerto Rican neighborhood: Rather than automatically extending credit to people who run up their phone bills, as they do in other areas, the company cuts off the long-distance phone service for customers in certain city blocks.

Racism is manifested in a variety of forms delineated below: prejudice, internalized oppression, discrimination, and institutionalized oppression.

Prejudice

Prejudice is the judgments we make about others without sufficient evidence to substantiate the opinions. Prejudice is like air; we can't help but breathe it in. We learn to be prejudiced from people who loved and raised us. We get messages from social, cultural, and religious sources:

- A billboard shows a strong, silent American Indian with a tear running down his cheek.
- Parents warn children about going into certain stores or playing with the kids who live in another part of town.
- Newspapers consistently show White men in suits and Black men wearing handcuffs.
- A minister talks about saving heathen babies in Africa.
- Television shows rarely feature Asian Americans, poor people, or people with disabilities.

Through these and other avenues, we learn about whom to consider important, who should play what roles, and whom society does not value.

Unexamined, these subtle and not so subtle messages shape our thinking about people. The anti-pollution commercial was one of the many images I saw as a child that portrayed American Indians as loving nature, being strong and silent, and existing only in a pseudo-historical context (wearing feathers and banging on drums). Today, in advertisements, movies, and conversations, I continue to see and hear portrayals of American Indians as caring only about nature, living in the past and not speaking up for themselves. Worse, many people talk as if American Indians are no longer alive. Thus, I have been powerfully trained to think that the American Indian student in my class will be quiet, nature loving, and "traditional"—a vague notion I can't even define! This is the prejudice I hold as a result of all the messages I have received since before I can remember. Marian, my student who identifies as a Seneca Indian, of course may be an avid punk rock fan who can't imagine leaving the city where she grew up and who talks loudly with her friends whenever she gets a chance.

Intersecting Identities

One's identity is not simply a matter of one's race. Activist and poet Audre Lorde (1984) explained that she is not a woman for part of the time, a lesbian at another time, a mother later, and Black on yet another occasion. Rather, she is all of them all the time. The aspects of our identities intersect and overlap. Consequently, it is not always possible to distinguish the reason for our prejudices. I may not know, for example, whether my perceptions of a student are because he is Puerto Rican, male, an atheist, a prize-winning chess player, or anything else. It is not possible for me to see him as separate from those aspects of his identity; he is all of those things. Although certain aspects of identity are more salient in certain times or places, no one element *inherently* trumps another.

Internalized Oppression

Prejudice can be so strong that we continue to hold inaccurate stereotypes even in the face of contrary evidence and even in instances when the stereotype applies to a group to which we belong. Unconsciously believing stereotypes about one's own group is called internalized oppression. I might rather have a male principal than a female principal because I have unconsciously internalized the idea that men are naturally better leaders than women are. I carry the prejudice even though I am a woman in a position of leadership, even though I know many women who are excellent leaders, and even though I know many men who are lousy leaders. Just because I am a woman does not mean that I am exempt from breathing the "air" of male superiority that circulates in the culture.

Internalized oppression should not be confused with what one does to survive or get ahead. A person who grew up in another country or in a working-class community may change her speech or dress to fit in with the corporate culture of her job. This does not necessarily mean that she is unconsciously ashamed of her ethnicity or socioeconomic background; she may be simply savvy enough to know what she needs to do to get ahead in her workplace.

Because we are not aware when we have internalized negative messages, internalized oppression is controversial. Would I think that my nose were too big if I had not grown up in a culture that continually perpetuates certain standards of beauty in magazines, television, and movies? Is it possible that the Black woman who straightens her hair is not concerned with gaining power in a particular environment, and has not internalized racism, but that she simply likes the look of straight hair? While many factors may explain our choices of hairstyle or principal, internalized oppression is not one of which we are aware, so it is difficult to know what effect it has.

Discrimination

Prejudice and internalized oppression are attitudes, thoughts, and feelings. Discrimination involves actions based on those prejudices. Discrimination can deny opportunity or stop people from being seen and treated as individuals. If, for example, I believe that red-haired people are violent and unpredictable, I might put my red-haired students in the back of the classroom. I might not take them on a field trip because I assume that they will not act appropriately. I am discriminating against those red-haired students. Similarly, I might believe that Asian Americans are good at math or that girls are good at creative writing. Based on those prejudices, I may not give the Asian American students in my algebra class the help they need, or I may not recognize the nonfiction writing skills of the girls in my language arts class. In all these cases, I am discriminating against my students.

Discrimination can be infuriating. For example, at a small university hotel, I talked with a visiting dignitary from Mexico who described what had happened her first morning there. The hotel served guests breakfast in a communal dining room. The dignitary went down for breakfast, and there was a man already seated at the table. When she approached, he asked her to get him a cup of tea. She explained that she did not work there. He did not seem even to hear her, insisting that she go get the tea he had requested. The man saw her skin color and gender and assumed that she could not possibly be a guest of the university. She and I were livid at this treatment.

Like prejudice, discrimination can be difficult to recognize. The man at the hotel might not have consciously meant to offend the Mexican dignitary. Nonetheless, his actions were not just demeaning. They were racist. His ignorance of his racism does not make it less racist. Correspondingly, racism would still have been at work even if the incident had not bothered the dignitary.

There is good reason to ask whether an employer choosing a particular job candidate, a new parent choosing a preschool, or a teenager choosing with whom to talk at a party is discriminating based on race. Discrimination comes with high, if hidden, price tags. In business, having employees with diverse experiences and outlooks allows a company to attack problems from a variety of angles and potentially better communicate with and serve its clients, the public, or its targeted market.

Similarly, the parent who seeks to shelter a child from those she doesn't know (assuming that the children will not share a certain value system or, worse yet, that the other children will teach her child undesirable values) does not help the child learn how to communicate with or learn from those who are different from him. Instead, she is modeling a fear of difference that can only limit the child's interactions with others.

Institutionalized Oppression

Institutionalized oppression is the systematic and systemic discrimination against people perceived to be in a certain group. My not calling on redheaded students is discrimination. If over and over again red-headed people are given fewer educational resources and less experienced teachers, denied access to certain jobs or decent health care, made to pay higher interest rates when they buy a car or a house, or discriminated against in the laws of the land, it is institutionalized oppression.

A shopowner may ask a person of color for two forms of identification when cashing a check, or a used-car salesperson may require a large down payment on a car from a person of color. Both may think they are simply using their judgment; but when they judge Whites to need only one form of ID or to have to pay a smaller down payment, they are discriminating. When the discrimination is part of the norms of organizations, it is oppression. Oppression is sometimes written into practice, as in the real estate formulas that compute higher interest rates for Latinos and African Americans than they do for Whites in comparable situations (Stuart, 2003).

There is a difference between individual acts of discrimination, based on prejudice, and institutional oppression, which, while carried out by individuals, has the weight of economic, political, social, or coercive power behind it. When a Latino woman is singled out at the airport and asked several questions about her travel before being allowed on the plane, it is not clear why she is being treated in such a manner. When the young security guard instructs his assistant to pull out the three more people with dark skin from the waiting line because he "doesn't like the look of them," it becomes apparent that this treatment is institutionalized oppression: discrimination multiplied by organizational power. Racial profiling of drivers, taxi drivers passing by certain customers, and tracking systems in schools that segregate most Whites from students of color are examples of ways in which discrimination is multiplied by the power of government, business, and educational institutions. Occurring within various systems and repeated over time, institutional oppression is more damaging than the discrete actions of individuals (Nieto, 2000).

Racism has been established and reinforced in laws throughout history. While southern states legalized the enslavement of Blacks, midwestern states also legislated discrimination. Indiana, Michigan, Iowa, and Wisconsin, for example, excluded Blacks from voting in the 1800s. Free Blacks could not live in Ohio without posting "a five-hundred dollar bond for good behavior," explains historian James Anderson (1994), and "in 1813 Illinois ordered every incoming free person of color to leave the territory under penalty of thirty-nine lashes, repeated every fifteen days until the African American left the state" (p. 94). In 2001, under the U. S. Patriot Act, many people of Middle Eastern descent were held in federal prisons or deported without proof of guilt (Leavitt, 2002).

Racism affects different communities in different ways. In 1882, the Chinese Exclusion Act discriminated against Chinese immigrants. Beyond the few stereotypical roles of geisha girl, karate expert, or math nerd, I didn't see many Asians in television, movies, or theater when I was growing up. More recently, Whites were hired to play the part of Asians in the Broadway play *Miss Saigon*. One director or producer alone did not decide not to hire Asians. Directors and producers reenacted and reinforced a long and particular history of oppression of Asians.

Discrimination carried out over numerous generations compounds institutionalized oppression. Producers want to hire big stars to draw crowds, but because of past discrimination, Asian Americans actors are not as well known as others. Therefore, they are not hired and they continue to be unemployed and invisible. Similarly, housing and educational admissions policies historically have discriminated against many groups. Networks available to Whites who were able to live in well-off neighborhoods and attend prestigious schools, and therefore to their children and grandchildren, are often lucrative in hidden ways (Roediger, 1999; Sugrue, 1999).

Moreover, there are collateral consequences of racism that are particularly damaging to individuals and communities of color (Travis, 2002). For instance, a Latino or Black man may be unfairly arrested and subsequently prosecuted, convicted, and sentenced to prison for a drug-related felony as a result of race-related discrimination (Blumstein, 1993; Spohn, 2000). He leaves prison only to discover that—even after serving his allotted time—federal law disqualifies him from obtaining federal education loans, serving on a jury, or joining the armed forces. In some states he even loses the right to vote ("Federal Statutes," n.d.; Chin, 2002). These consequences apply equally to all felons, but because of the initial discrimination, their effects are disproportionately felt in communities of color. As Toni Morrison (1992) points out, "Expensively kept, economically unsound, a spurious and useless political asset in election campaigns, racism is as healthy today as it was [centuries ago]" (p. 63).

White Privilege

In a racist system, Whites gain advantages because they are White (Apple, 1997; Frankenberg, 1993; Kincheloe & Steinberg, 1998; McIntosh, 1988; McLaren, 1997). Peggy McIntosh, a White professor of women's studies, has written a list of White privileges that includes, for instance, being free from harassment in a shopping mall and knowing that your race will not work against you in seeking medical treatment or public accommodation (McIntosh, 1988). White privilege relates to both individual and institutional racism. As a White person, I am not often stared at on the street of a predominantly White, midwestern town, for instance. I don't have to speak as a representative of my race, and I don't have undue trouble securing a reasonable bank loan.

The benefits of being White intersect with other privileges. I certainly accrue privilege as a result of my skin color, but my class status, gender, sexual orientation, age, and myriad other factors also mitigate and enhance my access to privilege. For example, McIntosh (1988) says that White privilege allows her to "go shopping alone most of the time, pretty well assured that [she] will not be followed or harassed." McIntosh's appearance and her status as a university professor, however, carry a unique mix of markers that are read in concert. Skin color is not the only factor affecting whether one will be perceived as a shoplifter. People who do not fit societal gender expectations, are dressed in tattered clothing, or have physical or mental disabilities are also often harassed.

Intersections of Oppressions

Oppressions overlap and intersect (Anzaldua, 1990; McCarthy & Crichlow, 1993; Wing, 1997). The history of toxic waste management provides an example of oppressions at work simultaneously. Ted Steinberg (2002), an environmental historian, explains that people of color have disproportionately been exposed to toxic waste in this country and that the institutional response to toxic dumping is related to race. He points to a 1992 study that showed that "fines imposed on polluters in White areas were, on average, more than five times the fines leveled on outlaws operating in minority communities" (p.256). In these cases, government regulators are responsible for institutionalized racism. So, too, are mainstream environmental organizations, which, for instance, have all but ignored serious radiation levels related to uranium mining on Navajo lands. "Were African Americans and other people of color literally being dumped on?" Steinberg asks. He cites government and other studies to show that they were. But, he adds, "It is also likely that toxic waste landfills, once sited, lowered surrounding land values, drawing those who lacked the means to live elsewhere to these areas" (p. 256). Race, class, and nationality combine in this instance to impact people's life chances.

Class and race also intersect in the ways in which people are able to accumulate wealth—a variable that often determines access to opportunity even more than income. Whites have been and continue to be able to accumulate wealth in ways denied to Blacks, Latinos, Native Americans, and Asian Americans (Sugrue, 1999). Because of inequitable real estate practices, Latinos, Blacks, and Native Americans have often not had access to homes in traditionally White (and often upscale) neighborhoods. When they have purchased homes in those neighborhoods, financial institutions then treat those areas as having lower property values (Williams, 1997a). Pulling oneself up by one's bootstraps is simply easier to do if you are White.

While there are many parallels between forms of oppression, learning about one form of oppression does not automatically mean that one can transfer the concepts, problems, or solutions to another kind of oppression. Learning about sexism, for example, can *help* students think about racism or homophobia, but students also need to address issues specific to a particular form of oppression. This is especially true if students have less experience addressing one kind of oppression than they do addressing another. Students also need to see how oppressions intersect and are compounded.

TEACHING ABOUT RACISM

For decades, educators have been concerned that students see positive images of various racial groups. Teachers and theorists have wanted students to think about and minimize the personal prejudice they feel toward people who are different from them (Banks, 1996). Many educators advocate that teachers do more than simply demand tolerance of differences or even celebrate diversity. They suggest that teachers should address the way oppressions intersect and are magnified by power. Education professor Lisa Delpit (1996) argues that teachers must explicitly teach students of color the rules of the culture of power so that these students can be successful in and beyond school. Many educators want students to understand institutionalized racism and the effects of discrimination for whole groups of people (Banks, 1997; Ladson-Billings, 1995; McCarthy & Willis, 1995; McIntosh, 1988; Nieto, 2000; Sleeter, 1993). Such educators feel it is important, particularly for White students, to help students see how Whites benefit from institutionalized racism (Fine et al., 1997; McIntosh, 1988).

Theorists often advocate more than one approach at once. Education professor James Banks (1997), for instance, offers a framework that starts with inclusion of content from various cultures, which he calls "content integration." Another dimension, "knowledge construction process," involves helping students determine how the cultural assumptions and racial positions of individuals and groups influence the creation of knowledge.

When I teach about Zimbabwe and other African kingdoms in my World History class, I am integrating content. When I describe the controversy over who got credit for building the fabulous structures in the Great Zimbabwe, I am helping students understand how knowledge is constructed. (Europeans were loath to acknowledge that the ruins at Zimbabwe represented an advanced civilization built by indigenous Africans, despite the overwhelming evidence that one existed. As late as 1970, the White Rhodesian government forced its official archaeologist to resign because he agreed that the ruins of the Great Zimbabwe were made by Africans [Stefoff, 1977].) Explaining the historiography helps students understand that history is constructed and is susceptible to the racist beliefs of those in power (M.E.K. Friends, personal communication, Mar. 22, 2003).

Another approach to understanding and combating racism in the classroom is to pay attention not just to the abstract notion of knowledge or rights, but also to everyday interactions among people. Several educators want teachers to conduct their classes so as to pay attention to inequitable social relations in the classroom itself (Apple, 1975; Ellsworth, 1989; Giroux & Pena, 1988). Who has more influence in discussions? How do teaching styles accommodate or alienate particular learners? How do teachers share or maintain their authority? (Banks, 1997; Cazden, 2001; Giroux & Pena, 1988; Ladson-Billings, 1997; C. Lewis, 2001).

Finally, there are educators who maintain that schools should teach students to actively fight for social change (Ayers, Hunt, & Quinn, 1998; Sleeter & McLaren, 1995; Stanley, 1992). Teachers and students should examine, challenge, and reconstruct the status quo of power dynamics in the classroom *and* in society. Fighting for social change "in the world" and working for equitable relations in the classroom are related. If we interact in equitable ways in the classroom, we are better able to constructively envision change in larger spheres. Knowing how to really hear what someone is saying and respond respectfully is the same skill whether we are talking face to face, or across continents. As Mahatma Gandhi is reputed to have counseled, "We must be the change we wish to see in the world."

CONCLUSION

By its nature, schooling involves careful investigation based on theory. We don't just have students run; we have them take their pulses and monitor their progress over time. We use the periodic table, the nutrition pyramid, and geometric theorems. Similarly, when we talk about race and racism, we need a theoretical foundation. Students should understand that race is a social and historical construction and that racism is multifaceted (personal as well as political and historical as well as current).

Understanding theory is critical to creating deeper conversations in the classroom. In order to make sense of the world, students need to be able to articulate what they see. How do race, class, gender, geography, and history affect one's position in the world and one's view of others? What institutional forces are at play? How does language shape our understanding? How do race and racism intersect with other aspects of identity and forms of oppression? What is the problem? Since students usually are not equipped with the analytical framework discussed in this chapter, part of our job is to supply the tools to build such a framework.

Racial literacy requires that students engage in interactions intellectually *and* emotionally. Students have to care about how race and racism affect them. They have to understand why they should pay attention and work for social change. Pricklier still, students and teachers have to learn how to interact with issues that are not always comfortable. Providing that guidance, however, is easier said than done. Academic strategies disconnected from real life are not enough to steer us through everyday conversations that are neither neat nor theoretical.

Seeing how students and teachers actually talk about race and racism in a real classroom puts flesh and muscles on the rather bare bones of theory. To that end, Chapter 3 introduces teachers Ann and Lewis and their second-period class. The students and teachers grappled with questions about race and racism. In Chapters 4, 5, and 6, I return to the theoretical framework in order to analyze their conversations and connect classroom practice to theory.

3

"How Come They Get Mad About the Cleveland Indians?" A Case Study of Discussions of Race and Racism in the Classroom

On the last day of the spring term, mayhem broke out in Ann Gerard and Lewis Shirer's interdisciplinary Language Arts/U.S. History class. Students shouted across the room. They argued whether the Atlanta Braves and the Jeep Cherokee were offensive names. Ann said that students were being racist. At one point in the discussion, she muttered in an audible aside, "I'm going to tell Lewis that we have failed." (Lewis, the other teacher in the class, was not there that day.)

The heated discussion began when Vic asked why Native Americans objected to the name of the baseball team the Cleveland Indians. Even when the class ended, the discussion did not have any neat resolution. As students put their folders away, Philip was still listing a trail of hypothetical sports teams: "the Kansas City Crackers," "the Georgia Jews."

From where I sat, the discussion was exciting. Far from having "failed," as Ann lamented, I thought that the conversation about popular culture was useful. Students had deliberated about the impact of racialized icons and language. I was delighted by the students' curiosity and energy. At the same time, I wondered what to make of the freewheeling discussion in which it was sometimes difficult to track a line of reasoning.

The class's debate about the Cleveland Indians is a good example of how, particularly when the subject was emotionally engaging, discussions could move quickly. The discussion is also an example of how conversations about race or racism could originate unexpectedly, when students or teachers picked up on a remark that was only tangentially related to the topic at hand. To give a sense of how the class looked and sounded, this chapter describes Ann and Lewis, the students, and the classroom, and then reconstructs sections of key class discussions from audiotapes of the classes. (Key discussions were those most heavily coded for race and racism when I analyzed the class transcripts.) Beyond minor clarifications, I present these selections as they occurred so that readers can see how students and teachers initiated conversations and batted topics around, sometimes inarticulately and sometimes elegantly.

U.S. HISTORY/LANGUAGE ARTS CLASS

Ann and Lewis's 80-minute, second-period class started at 8:30 in the morning. Students, often carrying bottles of orange juice or soda, retrieved their class folders from a tall filing cabinet and found seats around eight rectangular tables arranged in a large open square. (When a student complained that folders were missing, Ann joked, "They sell 'em. . . . You could fetch a high price for these folders!") This was the third term of a year-long course. The atmosphere of the class, like the room itself, was stimulating but also casual. Students called the teachers by their first names, as was customary in the school.

The room was colorful and cluttered. Posters of bullfighters contrasted with the dull green chalkboards and dark gray speckled industrial carpeting. Rolling bookshelves held a hodge-podge of literature and American history textbooks, poetry books, dictionaries, and faded paperback novels. Folders, notebooks, coffee mugs, videotapes, library books, and boxes of magazines and crayons covered Ann's large wooden desk and the counter in the back of the room.

I was a visitor in this class, an observer trying to find out more about how students and teachers talk about race and racism. I sat at the tables with the teachers and students. Occasionally, I asked questions or gave my response to a general prompt. (Lewis had suggested that the students would trust me more if I participated in the class to some degree rather than simply watching and taking notes.) I was friendly with the students, but I usually refrained from stating my opinion about the topic of class discussion because I wanted students to feel as free as possible to tell me what they thought. After the first couple of weeks, once the students had gotten to know me, I obtained everyone's permission, set up a tape recorder on the table, and recorded the discussions.

The Students

In the course of the term, I came to grow fond of the somewhat rambunctious teenagers, many of whom participated regularly in class discussions:

- Edmund, the charismatic 17 year-old Black student who wanted to be a lawyer
- Tim, the preppy-looking White senior who DJ'd at hip-hop events
- Philip, the wiry, redheaded young White man who was learning Chinese at the local community college
- Vic, the self-described "goofy" Asian student, who always wore shorts to class, no matter what the weather
- Leslie, the rather serious White girl, whom Ann described as "consciously counterculture"
- Antoine, the tall African American boy who was quick to flash a bright, youthful smile as he looked over at my laptop computer and asked if I was writing about him
- Tricia, the bouncy White student whose Valley Girl speech belied her curiosity and intensity
- Jake, the muscular, opinionated White boy who started the term with quarter-inch blond hair but soon shaved it off in anticipation of joining the military after graduation

Other students were quieter, but the teachers consistently tried to draw all students into discussions. Of the 24 students registered for the class, 18 identified themselves as White, 3 as Black, and 1 each as Chicano, Asian, and mixed Black and White. Because of sporadic attendance patterns, there were usually about 12 to 15 students in class each day. Those students were mostly boys and mostly juniors and seniors. (See Appendix A for a chart of all the participants in the class.)

The Teachers

The teachers in the class were Ann Gerard and Lewis Shirer. Ann was a 65-year-old, middle-class White teacher who had taught Language Arts at Central High School for 22 years. She also co-directed the school's drama program. Ann had grown up in various parts of the United States. She had straight salt-and-pepper hair down to just below her ears, and she dressed casually—often in jeans and a sweater or brightly colored T-shirt. One of the students in the class said that Ann was "kind of quiet until something stirs her up." But, he added, "I guess anyone seems reserved next to Lewis."

Lewis, a 49-year-old Black teacher, grew up in what he called a "working poor" family in Alabama. Lewis had taught social studies at Central for 8 years. He also coached football at one of the local comprehensive high schools. Before teaching, Lewis had worked as an Equal Opportunity Coordinator for a large industrial corporation for 18 years. He had short black-and-white hair and a close-cropped white beard and moustache. He, too, dressed casually—often in khaki trousers, a Central T-shirt, and black athletic shoes.

Ann and Lewis had been team-teaching this interdisciplinary Language Arts and U.S. History class since the beginning of the year, and most of the students had been with them for one or both of the previous trimesters. Both teachers used a sense of humor to push students to accomplish intellectual tasks. Ann smiled easily. People who met her for the first time often mistook her for being quiet, even deferential. Lewis appreciated her wisdom and her measured approach: "She has insight. She's so evenhanded, you know." Lewis's humor was often dry. He followed his jokes and jibes with a hearty laugh. Lewis often told stories from his own experience to illustrate a point, and students would listen attentively. Ann said of him: "I think Lewis is sort of the preacher, [a] storyteller."

INTRODUCING RACIAL TOPICS

Several times throughout the term, Ann and Lewis specifically initiated discussions about race and racism. They asked students to analyze a section of the video *Simple Justice* (Brandt et al., 1993), a television documentary about the *Brown v. Board of Education of Topeka, Kansas* court case. They had students practice reading skills with "The Tonto Syndrome" (1989), an article about how Whites are given top billing in different media. In the examples that follow, teachers introduced discussions about racial topics with a question and a poem. In both of these discussions, students and teachers together built on the questions and materials presented.

Journal Question: "What Does Civil Rights Mean?"

Before beginning a unit on the 1960s, Lewis wrote two questions on the board: "What does civil rights mean? What does it mean to have your civil rights violated?" The ensuing discussion was what Ann and Lewis called a "journal discussion." Ann or Lewis would start the class with a question that either got students to think about the issues that they would be studying or to reflect on what they had covered. Students would write about the question in their journal notebooks for about 10 minutes and then take turns explaining their answers.

At the beginning of the class students seemed to agree that civil rights were accorded to everyone equally. When Lewis invited students to talk in terms of particular groups, the discussion involved controversy about labels and definitions. The class grappled with the questions of who gets to have rights, at what age, and in what countries. In this conversation, the class's attention shifted from one topic to another. The students sometimes ignored salient points. Then a question of terminology deflected the students' attention.

"What are we familiar with in this country?" Lewis probed. "Have you ever heard the term *civil rights* being used in connection with a group?"

"Yeah," Jake offered, "the colored people and the—"

"The who?!" Lewis interrupted.

"Colored people and women," Jake continued.

"The colored people and women," Lewis repeated, disconcerted by Jake's language.

"Are [the two main parts] of the struggle of civil rights in our country," Jake finished.

"You mean?" Tricia began. "What do you mean?"

Several students talked at once.

Lewis repeated the question: "Have you heard the term *civil rights* in conjunction with a group? Jake said 'colored people and women.' You probably mean 'people of color,' right?"

"Yeah," replied Jake.

"That's what you [meant]," Lewis confirmed.

Students laughed. Their laughter seemed to me to be at Jake for using the term *colored people*, but it also seemed like nervous laughter. Hank, a soft-spoken boy with fine blond hair, was taken aback.

"He said *colored people*!" Hank said quietly to the student next to him.

"People of color and women," Lewis announced, and then immediately focused again on his question about rights. "But you told me they were rights given to you as Americans. So, so, does that track?" he asked, wondering whether civil rights applied to only some people or to all Americans.

Edmund responded: "It doesn't mean colored people or women as American, but usually more often than not they get discriminated against and have to fight for your civil rights."

Colored people was clearly a loaded term for the class, although when Edmund used the phrase there was no response. The conversation continued with Lewis picking up on the mention of civil rights: "'Fight for my civil rights.' What does that mean?"

"If your civil rights were violated," Edmund explained, "if you're, like, discriminated against, if, like, for any reason, for your color, for your gender, it's more likely to happen to a Black man or a White female than a White male."

"OK, you said a couple things. You said *discriminated* against." Lewis wrote the word on the board as he spoke. "What does that mean?" Lewis was leading the class to tentative definitions of civil rights and discrimination that he thought they would need as they began researching the 1960s, their next assignment.

Although we often nudge students in certain directions, it is impossible for teachers to know in advance where students will go with questions such as these. Just as the class was coming to the notion that discrimination meant being looked down on or treated unequally because of one's race or gender, Tricia complicated the class consensus: "I just want to say that I think it goes a lot, like way deeper than just race and sex. There has to be some discrimination, some civil rights that are fought by people who, don't, like—I don't want to say poor people." She paused, monitoring her words. "People who don't have as much money as other people. Like sometimes."

"And then," she added, "like now there's so many more like unique individuals, like doing their own thing. I think that if you dress differently, you have to kind of fight for your civil rights 'cause you might get discriminated against because of how you dress or act."

Lewis did not directly address Tricia's reference to discrimination based on socioeconomic class. Instead, he moved the conversation in another direction to get at an understanding of what discrimination looks like: "How do I know if I'm being discriminated against?"

"It's not hard to tell," said Edmund.

"It is?!" Lewis asked, his feigned surprise an encouragement for the students to give more details.

"Well, like what if you went into a restaurant and you weren't like everybody else and you didn't get a server, and you sat there for an hour and nobody came to your table?" Tricia offered.

Lewis picked up on the idea: "OK, so I'm going to be treated differently in a restaurant because I'm not like everybody else. So discrimination is being treated differently because I'm not like everybody else. [Do you] buy into that?"

"I'll buy it," Philip responded clearly. "I agree with that."

"Well, if I'm a male, I would get treated different because I'm a Black male?" Lewis prodded. The students were silent. "So would that tend to be not because of my maleness, but because of what else?"

"Color," a few students called out.

"My color!" Lewis agreed.

"But in some places you can go into a place and get discriminated against 'cause you're a White male," Edmund posited, shifting his argument.

Within several minutes, the class discussion had moved from a general definition of civil rights as those that apply to all people or all Americans to a more particular examination of the ways in which groups of people are more likely to experience discrimination or enjoy rights. At the end, however, several students argued that anyone could be discriminated against at any time. Lewis weaved and bobbed around the topics, sometimes following the students' leads, and sometimes choosing his own direction.

"Poem for the Young White Man . . ."

A few days after their introductory conversation about civil rights, the teachers used a poem to initiate discussion. Steve Cervantes, another teacher in the school, had suggested Lorna Dee Cervantes' (1990) "Poem for the Young White Man Who Asked Me How I, an Intelligent, Well-Read Person, Could Believe in the War Between Races" to Lewis. Lewis invited Steve to join the class to share the poem with the students. Students' responses to the poem involved quite a bit of student-to-student interaction.

Steve began by introducing the notion of race as a significant factor: "Before we start this poem, one thing that's kind of interesting about it is that it shows that between different people, people who look different, other races—whether race is real or not—people of different races tend to have really different perspectives. You know." In his aside, Steve touched on the debate over whether or not race is a biological fact, but he did not elaborate. He went on to cite an example of how people in different groups view television shows. "What's the top-rated show on TV? *ER*, overall. Among African Americans, it's [number] 42 or something."

"Mm-hmm," Edmund agreed.

"Just think about that," Steve continued. "The shows that are top-rated among— by European Americans are really not [rated the same] by other groups. You just have to think about that. It's really stunning."

A few of the students talked about how they might rate *ER*. Vic said he would not think of it as number 1.

"I've seen *ER* once." Edmund offered. "It's a pretty good show, but it just doesn't catch [my] attention all the time." Several students talked to each other about their television preferences.

"So," Steve said, getting the students back to his point, "this poem shows how different people have completely different perspectives."

After four volunteers read the poem (reprinted in Appendix B) to the class, Steve complimented the readers, and then asked if there were any lines that jumped out at the students.

"Is the purpose of the poem to explain to the young White man what it's like to be not White in the world today?" Philip asked.

"Is that what you think?" Steve replied.

"Is it?" Philip repeated.

"With poetry it's what you interpret," Edmund offered confidently. "'Cause what he's gonna interpret is gonna be so much different. Because, like, what I interpret, you know maybe you could see that." Edmund spoke assertively, particularly as he addressed the explicitly racial element of the poem: "But I can see from this poem you'll never understand. A young White man will never understand, not by reading this poem, what it's like to be a young Black man." In his statement, Edmund posited a gulf between Black and White understandings.

"But it says 'Poem for the Young White Man,'" Philip countered. The statements hung in the air.

After a moment, Antoine reread the title: "For the young White man who asked me how I da da da."

Tabitha jumped in, "I think it's more of a way to get everybody to open up in their life that it doesn't matter what color you are—there's still someone out there who can hear you. Even though I'm White, he's Oriental (pointing to Vic), and he's mulatto (pointing at Edmund)."

Once again, language was at issue. "Oriental is a rug!" Vic objected. Then several other students spoke out at once. I could only make out phrases in their overlapping voices: "Oriental is not—" "Something from the Orient." "Asian." "Oriental is a thing."

"I'm just saying!" Tabitha protested above the din.

"Adults told me not to call it Oriental," Vic explained amid the talk.

"She's pointing at you," Antoine reported to Edmund.

"Get it straight," Edmund responded. "I'm Black—100%!"

The students continued to call out, reacting to Tabitha's language:

"When I was a young kid, adults told me not to call it 'Oriental,'" Vic explained loudly to no one in particular.

"Oriental is the food," Edmund announced.

"Orient is something from the Orient," said Philip.

"It's like a thing," Vic added.

"Mulatto?!" Richard exclaimed.

Thinking about the term, Hank leaned over and asked me, "Isn't there a possibility that there was a Black man in my family?"

As often happened, the discussion moved in an unforeseen direction. The digression served to open the question of racial appellations. Students touched on the problem of naming that Edward Said (1978) described in *Orientalism*. However, it was hard to tell whether Tabitha and others achieved greater understanding. As I listened, I felt protective of Tabitha, worrying that she might be shamed into silence. Yet I also knew that it was important for her to understand why some words might offend people. Other students in the class could probably also learn from the students' excited reactions.

Philip wanted to look up *Orient* in the dictionary, but Lewis deterred him. "Not to squash your wanting to know," Lewis told Philip, "but it's like we need to move on." Students continued talking on the side about the terms. Lewis explained, "We also need to acknowledge the fact that we have various— We have a salad here. Various—" He paused. "Think of it as a salad. This room is like a salad. We have various—" He didn't finish his sentence. A student read a line from the poem, and the class moved on.

"I didn't get it," Vic admitted.

Edmund interpreted, "Like one time in this class somebody said that you, [Lewis], like sometimes you, like, take racial issues, like, too far, and look at 'em too much. But, you know, like it says right here, 'I know you don't believe this. You think this is nothing but a faddish exaggeration. But they are not shooting at you.' Then it's like— I forgot where it was. There's another part in here about, uh—"

The students were unusually silent as Edmund looked for the section he wanted. He continued, "It says— I can't remember where it was— it's just like— It says like they go and hide and, like, they pretend like they can't—"

The teachers, students, and I were listening intensely, each of us silently filling in the blanks and guessing at innuendos. Discussions like these are difficult to facilitate because often we do not stop to identify inconsistencies or omissions. I wanted to slow the discussion down and examine students' words and meanings, but at the same time, I didn't want to get in the way of the flow of the dialogue.

After a pause, several students talked at once. Lewis spoke over them: "Can I ask you a question about the racial issue? Sometimes I wonder if I was White and if I had been trying to be open and not be accused of those things, how would I feel if every time you see something, you see Blacks being put upon by Whites? Every time you mention the word there's a negative connotation. I wonder about that."

Lewis did not wait long for an answer. Perhaps answering his own question about being White, he went on to connect being accused of racism to a larger theme that he often talked about: American history as an ongoing experiment in democracy. "I think we need to understand where we came from as a nation. And again, here we go with this experiment. Not everybody has been on the side of [a] right and clear divide. So, *please* don't feel put upon because of who you are. Please don't feel that. If *ever* you feel that you've been picked on just because of who you are we need to know that."

Leslie and Philip raised their hands and kept them up, a move that was unusual in this class, where the teachers did not want to have to give permission for students to talk.

"I'm not saying that," Edmund said to Lewis.

"I hear where you're coming from," Lewis continued. "I'm saying that has crossed my mind several times. Because some people might say, 'Well, here we go again, talking about how bad the White people are.'"

Lewis and Edmund seemed to be talking at cross-purposes. Edmund had begun by recalling an accusation that Lewis talked too much about race. Edmund was using the poem to defend Lewis' talking about race. Lewis, concerned that students might feel defensive, reassured the class that he was not saying that the Whites in the class were being blamed.

Seeming to ignore Lewis's fear about Whites or others being stereotyped or criticized, Edmund picked up his copy of the poem and pressed on with his point, using his own experience to prove that racism exists: "I don't think we're talking about this one right here. She says: 'I'm not a revolutionary. / I don't like political poems. / Do you think I can believe in a war between races? / I can deny it. I can forget about it / when I'm safe / living in my own continent of harmony / at home, but I am not / there' [*sic*]."

"You know sometimes, I've seen people, like, try to push it back and forget about it: Well, I can forget about it and deny it, and then it's not happening, you know? But it doesn't work like that! You know? That's what I see. Sometimes just observing people you can tell that they do that, you know? They don't want to talk about it as much. They want to push it back. Like some of the people I hang around with sometimes. It's always there! But some people try to avoid it but it doesn't work 'cause it'll still be there regardless." It was not unusual for Edmund to be argumentative or confrontational, but his examples here were remarkably personal. The poem clearly struck a chord with students.

EXPANDING THE CONVERSATIONS

The introduction of the provocative poem led almost immediately to students and teachers broadening the discussion beyond the concrete material of the poem and into their own lives. During the term, I saw students and teachers lead conversations to new arenas in several impromptu ways, sometimes directly related to the topic at hand and sometimes only tangentially related:

- They told stories—anecdotes heard elsewhere and stories of students' own personal experiences—as you will see in the continuation of the discussion of the poem and in a conversation about freedoms guaranteed to American citizens.
- Their experiences included references to popular culture, such as in a discussion of censorship on television and the discussion of the Cleveland Indians.
- They talked about current events and trends such as in a conversation about police profiling.

To illustrate these expansions, I return to the discussion of the poem and then describe four other key discussions.

Stories About Stereotypes: "Hit the Floor!"

While Edmund was quoting the poem and talking about his acquaintances who denied the existence of racism, Leslie had kept her hand up, ready to object. When he finished, Leslie dove into the conversation, with an anecdote to explain her position that racism is not a problem. "OK, I would like to say that, OK, it's not necessarily [a problem]." But then she continued: "I think things are somewhat turning around. Like everybody always talks about 'Oh, the Whites did such and such to the Blacks.' Yeah. No shit. You know. That sucks and everything. But, like there was this lady who came to [my old school] this one time and she was like, 'Oh, you did this to me. You guys enslaved me.' And I was like 'Fuck you! I didn't do anything to you.' I wasn't even born. I wasn't an idea."

One of the students made a joke I couldn't hear and several students laughed.

Edmund responded to Leslie's complaint that people have unfairly accused her of racist acts: "See, that's some people's, like, own downfall."

"That's a person with a chip on their shoulder," Vic said at nearly the same time.

"I don't blame anybody I know now," Edmund elaborated. "I don't blame any of the White people that are alive now, but I do have beef with the people who are still out there running around with White sheets over their head, you know, burning crosses. But, like, you, I would *never* hate you for what happened 400 years ago. That's other people's hang-ups. They think they have an excuse to blame other people because their ancestors were enslaved. It's a lot different."

"Would you say there's something that's going on that's happened as a result of that?" Lewis asked, and explained that people might still be advantaged by systems set up long ago.

"Yeah," Edmund replied, "but then you can't be mad because we were enslaved 400 years ago. Be mad at what's still happening as a result of that."

In response to Edmund's suggestion that people "be mad at what's still happening as a result of [slavery]," Ann told an anecdote about racism today that she had heard at a conference. The presenter at the conference, Ann recalled, "told about a woman who was a well-dressed White woman, who got on an elevator in, I don't know, some big city. And she got on and was not paying too much attention about what was happening, and stood there for a little while, and some more people got on, and some more people got on. And she looked kind of out of the corner of her eye and saw three very, very tall Black men standing kind of behind her."

"Colored folk," Antoine said, filling out Ann's explanation with his own nomenclature.

Ann continued: "They had just gotten on the elevator. They had on jackets and hats,"

"She quick moved her purse," a student predicted, surmising that the White woman would be afraid of being robbed by the Black men.

Ann continued: "And one of them said, 'Hit the floor.' And [the woman] panicked. And she fell down on the floor. And when [the presenter] was telling this, he was just having fun with it."

Ann interrupted herself, mimicking the presenter's astonishment: "'She fell down on the floor!'"

In her own voice, Ann continued the story about the woman in the elevator. "And she was really having a fit. And she looked up and they were all laughing, kind of like 'what's going on here?' What *they* [the Black men] meant was push the button for the floor on the elevator."

The students laughed.

Ann continued with the end of the story. "And then later on [the woman] was sitting in the restaurant, and the waiter brought over a bottle of . . . some really expensive champagne and put it in front of her, and she said, 'What's this for?' And he said, 'Well, it's from that gentleman over there.' They were all wearing suits. And it was three— um, it was Dennis Rodman was one of them (which you think she'd recognize) and then two other players from—"

"The Bulls?" a student offered.

Ann nodded. "It was when Chicago was still [a championship team.] And they put a little note [with the bottle] and they said, 'Thank you for one of the best laughs I've ever had, but'—I don't remember his exact words—'be careful about making judgments.'"

Ann went on to explain her point: "But I think that's where, you know, we all think that we've come a long way, but you do have to—." The end of her sentence was lost amid the eruption of students' talk. "She still had that fear," Ann added, explaining how the White woman in the elevator had been afraid of the Black men.

The anecdote (which I had heard before and assumed was an urban legend) was Ann's response to Edmund, Lewis, and Leslie talking about what is happening as a result of slavery. I am not sure that the class saw the connection between the dehumanization of Blacks in slavery and the woman's fear of the Black men in the elevator—that in order to defend the inhuman practice of slavery, Whites dehumanized Blacks and claimed that they needed to be feared. Nonetheless, the story focused the conversation on current forms of racism. Students responded by addressing how stereotypes work.

Several students began talking at once. "You hear about it all the time," Leslie said, "but, even though you're told that it's wrong—"

"What'd you say, Leslie?" I asked over the talk.

"Partially maybe that could be because we're taught it, even though we're taught that it's wrong."

"What are we taught?" I asked.

"How are we taught?" Ann added.

"[That] all the Black people are—" Leslie started.

"Gonna rob you," Edmund finished her sentence.

"But that a lot of times could be true, too," Tim objected. "Depends on where you go and what you do in life."

"And who you are!" Edmund added.

"Stereotypes can usually be mostly right," Leslie said. "Well, it depends on your stereotypes, but some of them—." The students went on to explore stories of situations when their own stereotypes had and had not been accurate. The conversation that had begun with the reading of a poem had taken the class in several directions.

Popular Culture: "They Can't Show Guns on BET."

Although the teachers initiated most conversations about race and racism, students also raised and extended these issues. In one discussion, students used popular culture as well as their own opinions and personal examples to talk about ways in which race and socioeconomic status affect one's independence. The class had begun with a journal question: "Name and describe at least three freedoms we are guaranteed as Americans."

"You have a right to buy a gun," a student proclaimed in response to the prompt.

"That's guaranteed," Philip qualified, "if you don't have a record, and you are middle aged, and you're White."

"They are freedoms but they are not guaranteed." Cliff jumped in. "Like they say people are equal, but in the South—"

Lewis responded by directing them from particular examples of freedoms to the source of the supposed freedoms: "Where do they say that?"

"In the Constitution," a chorus of students responded.

"'All men are created equal,'" Cliff said, quoting the Declaration of Independence.

"'All men'" Lewis repeated pointedly. "That's it right there!" he added, alluding to the fact that the original documents referred only to land-owning White men.

Discussing freedom of speech and censorship, Philip argued that a song about someone shooting himself with a gun would be allowed to air on television if it were a song that was alternative. "On TV, I saw the MTV censor. Alternative music is allowed. Rap and hip-hop are watched so much more closely than alternative [music]."

Thinking that more musicians considered alternative were White than those considered hip-hop or rap, I asked why such distinctions were made. Several students talked at once.

"[Rap is censored] because it's more widespread," Edmund suggested.

"There are more young people listening now," Tim added. "But how can you restrict one person and not another person?" he asked amid the cacophony of excited student talk.

"Can they say it on BET [Black Entertainment Television]?" Philip asked, referring to the mention of guns.

"They can't show guns on BET," Edmund responded.

The discussion was fast-paced. Students circled around the question of censorship by referencing popular culture. Although it had seemed to me at first that they were leaping from topic to topic, they were actually getting at bigger ideas of freedom. They made tacit connections. By bringing up BET, Philip raised the issue of race.

I followed up with a question: "Do you think there's an element of race [in the censorship]?"

"Slim Shady's White," Tim and Edmund answered simultaneously. Slim Shady, otherwise known as Eminem, is a popular singer who is White.

The conversation about freedoms swirled on. The students went on to use their own as well as stories from the media to make sense of the impact of race, class, and gender. Jeremy mentioned that in some places people are not free to dress the way they want.

"So move," Vic quipped, suggesting that if people do not feel free to dress as they like, they should go and live where they feel less inhibited.

"Some people don't have the means [to move]," Edmund countered.

I asked if the guarantee of freedom was related to money. Flores nodded.

Edmund related that his friend, "a White girl in a brand new [expensive car]," never gets a ticket when she commits a traffic violation. He compared her experience to the way the police had treated him: "Me and Flores in a beat-up Taurus: we get pulled over." He held up his hands as if he were being frisked. "Got given every ticket in the book." Edmund's contrast of two young men, one Black and one Chicano, driving a cheap car with the White girl driving an expensive one demonstrated how aspects of identity overlap.

In an effort to sort out whether the privileges some people enjoyed were due to their race, socioeconomic status, or fame, Tricia brought up the case of O. J. Simpson and wondered if money was the trump card in attaining freedom.

"He didn't do it," Jake stated, poker-faced. The class laughed and the conversation about freedoms ended. Although Tricia had opened the door, no one wanted to touch the charged controversy of the Simpson trial after Jake's joke.

In this conversation, students and teachers moved easily between their own personal experiences and references to popular culture. Indeed, distinguishing between personal experience and popular culture is artificial: Popular culture is part of our personal experiences.

Cleveland Indians Discussion

Another example of students' leadership in discussions about race was in the conversation about the Cleveland Indians described at the beginning of this chapter. Vic's question about Native Americans getting mad about the name of the Cleveland Indians was a surprising but provocative tangent to the discussion. Vic had been giving a report about the populations and employment of Native Americans in the United States. His abrupt question triggered strong reactions.

Another student, Peter, wondered, "How come they get mad about the Cleveland Indians but not the Jeep Cherokee?" The boys (there were no girls in the class that day) loudly discussed the names. They laughed and said the caricatures used by sports teams were not racist.

Ann disagreed.

Vic, who identified himself as Asian or Korean, said that if someone took a fat Buddha and called a team the Buddhists he would not be offended.

The class's prevailing sentiment was that logos such as the Cleveland Indians' and other cartoon depictions were not insulting. Two students gave counterexamples: One held that turning the Fat Albert character into a logo would be offensive, and another described some of the portrayals of Blacks in Japanese cartoons as racist.

In the midst of this argument about logos and racism, Philip, Edmund, and Vic discussed their discomfort with forms that ask them to check off their race in a box.

"I don't want to be called 'White,'" announced Philip.

"I check 'other,'" Edmund replied and laughed.

"How come we don't just all be American?" asked Vic.

In the course of this prickly argument, students deliberated about the impact of racialized icons and language, and they examined, albeit briefly, the practice of distinguishing people by race. In this case, a student had directed the conversation to questions of race. In the next example, Lewis and I were responsible for shifting the focus of the discussion. We asked questions to try to get students to think about who gets sent to prisons, and the nature of the justice system in general.

Current Events: "I Get Followed, Too!"

On a somewhat sleepy morning, in preparation for a unit on the Vietnam War, Lewis wrote the journal question on the board: "Who do you think should fight when your country's at war?"

In the ensuing discussion, Malik suggested that prisoners be sent to war: "What's the point of keepin' 'em here if we need help fighting a war and they had this problem of people not wanting to go? You want to pay for somebody to stay in prison?"

"For one thing," Ann replied, "I think it'd be very illegal. And the other thing is— One of the reasons you put people in prison is to rehabilitate 'em."

Malik laughed at the idea. Several students started talking at once.

I wondered about the racial implications of prisoners being sent to war. From the beginning of the term, Ann and Lewis had encouraged me to jump into the conversation at any time. I rarely did, but on this occasion I was curious about how the students might deal with this question. "Who gets put in prison?" I asked.

"Yeah," Ann said emphatically, reinforcing my question. "There you go."

Students suggested that people in prisons were criminals.

"The ones that get caught," Malik smiled.

"The stupid ones?" another student asked, half-joking. Several students laughed.

"Is it the stupid ones who get caught?" I asked.

After some more discussion about innocence, guilt, and murder, Lewis asked, "Well, who is the biggest majority of people in [this state's] prisons?" His direct question got the students to think about the prison population in terms of race.

"Black folk," Malik answered.

"Black males," Lewis confirmed.

Many students talked at once. "That's the majority," one said.

Edmund and Lewis made guesses about the percentage of Blacks in the state, both contending that it was a small minority. Tim then asked a question to challenge the assertion that Blacks were disproportionately imprisoned: "Does that have anything to do with the fact that there might be more Black criminals in Riverville?"

Lewis used a personal story to refute the idea. "Would there be [more Black criminals? Or] would it be the fact that I'm more likely to get stopped?

"Mmm-hmm," agreed Edmund.

Lewis explained what had happened to him one day on the way to school: "I drove to school up here. Police followed me. I'm coming to school. Would George Doyle [a White teacher] be stopped? I don't know."

"I get followed, too!" Tim cried out. "I get followed, too!" His words got covered by many other students talking at once. "Wouldn't that be [that] there's more Black people in jail in Riverville, so wouldn't that mean there's more Black criminals in Riverville?" Tim continued. "Or do you think that you guys just get fucked with more?" he asked, directing his question at Lewis.

Once again, many students talked at once. "The majority of the people in prison in [this state] for violent crimes are White people," Edmund said clearly. "The majority of the Black people in prison in [this state] are in there for crimes like—"

"Drugs," Tim finished Edmund's sentence.

The students debated whether more Blacks did drugs than other people did. As I listened, I wished that they had accurate statistics with which they could debate these questions.

"I think it does have to do with being caught," Ann claimed, going back to the question of police stopping motorists. "I think that there's some studies, Tim, that are really kind of interesting. It really does have to do with being picked up and caught."

Several students talked at once about whom the police pull over. "But I get pulled over, too, man," Tim continued to argue. "Like I get followed and I get messed with, too."

The class's tug-of-war conversation echoed the debate over racial profiling that was taking place publicly around the country. Why is there a disproportionate number of Black people in prisons? The class went on to complicate the racial question with deliberations of age and gender.

"What kind of car do you drive?" Ann asked Tim.

"A Geo."

"Well, that doesn't fit too well." Ann had guessed that, like many other Central High School students, Tim might be driving a particular kind of beat-up car, and that he would have been stopped by police because he is a teenager. "I was gonna say I think also young people get pulled over." She did not address the fact that Tim would have to have access to some wealth to drive as nice a car as a Geo, but several students took up the idea that young people might be discriminated against more than others.

"Yeah, we are followed, too," Hank acknowledged. "But, you know, even though you may not realize it, but Black people are, like, followed by cops. They do get stopped more."

Tim continued asserting his position amid many students' arguments.

"White males do get harassed as much," Edmund said, turning from his original position, "but I know a lot of White girls who in a minute will get off."

"Yes, I admit it!" Josh said, "I get off because I'm White."

"Asian girls get off," Vic added. "My sister gets off all the time." With these few comments, the boys deflected the escalating conflict.

Once again, students and teachers had broadened the conversation in a number of directions. The discursive discussion went from concentrating on race to wondering about how class, age, and gender also affect interactions with police officers. In a disjointed fashion, the students were posing complicated questions. Many students talked animatedly.

In these conversations, students responded to questions about race. At other times, however, students or teachers asked questions, made comments, or brought up topics related to race or racism and others in the class did *not* respond. The next section describes some of those incidents.

IGNORED REFERENCES

The class dealt with many topics other than race and racism. There were also many times when they ignored those subjects. This section describes a few of the times when references or questions about race—even those that were clearly related to the topic at hand—were disregarded.

On the first day of the term, Lewis asked the students to introduce themselves. When his turn came, Vic let out a slight giggle and said he was "the Amazing Asian." He did not say anything else and the others continued around the table. I thought it was an odd comment, but assumed that it was an inside joke among the students, who had been together for the previous 6 months of the school year.

A little while later, when the class was brainstorming what they knew about the United States in the 1950s, Vic laughed as he offered "the Korean War."

"Why are you laughing?" Lewis asked.

"'Cause I'm Korean," he replied. No one said anything else about his laughter. The references to race were briefly placed on the table, noticed by some perhaps, but not picked up.

As it turned out, Vic often made comments or asked questions about race. Sometimes, as in the discussion of the Cleveland Indians, students responded: At other times, students and teachers ignored the references. During the discussion of the poem, Vic said that he had gotten beaten up in a store because he was Asian. Although it was an audible aside, no one responded to the comment.

References such as an off-the-cuff joke or a physical description were unlikely segues to conversations about race or racism. One day, for example, Philip was setting up the video projector. Jake, who has blond hair and fair white skin, was sitting in the front of the room, directly in the line of the projector. "It's good that Jake is so white," Philip joked, "because we're now going to project [the video] on you." Skin color was the basis of a joke, and nothing more was said about it.

At other times, students used race to describe people. One day in the beginning of May, Antoine bounded into the room. He said that his stomach was upset and he wondered if I would buy him a Coke. "I need some Milk of Magnesia," he said loudly. He laughed and asked anyone who was listening, "You seen that commercial? That Maalox commercial? That Black lady is always like 'My boy uses it all the time,'" imitating the speaker in a high-pitched voice. When Antoine referred to the fact that the woman on the commercial was Black, no one stopped him to investigate his comment. It didn't seem like there was any need to do so.

Later on in that period, however, students talked about race in ways that were less neutral. At the end of the class period when students had talked about who should go to war, students talked informally before leaving the room.

Antoine looked at Vic, the only Asian American in the class, and jibed, "I think all the Asians should go."

Vic retorted with a joke: "'Cause we're like Ninjas."

Some students laughed.

Ann let out a big sigh but did not respond.

"How can you tell the difference in war?" Vic asked after a minute. "Shoot, I'd be shooting everyone with slanted eyes."

No one said anything more about Asians or war. Students got up to put away their folders and started talking about their favorite Chinese foods. Vic's words haunted me. That none of us in the room responded with more than a sigh or a laugh was equally haunting.

As these examples show, students mentioned race in everyday talk. Sometimes there seemed to be nothing wrong with letting remarks go without comment. At other times, however, the disregard troubled me. I was determined to investigate the reasons why the class would ignore such comments.

CONCLUSION

There was no predetermined script to follow when teachers and students talked about race and racism. Topics ranged from analysis of terms to reactions to literature to discussions of current controversies. Sometimes students and teachers investigated topics carefully; sometimes they just mentioned them. It sometimes felt like I was watching a Ping-Pong game with several balls in play at once. Conversations often ricocheted in many directions, with students expressing heated opinions. Why were some conversations superficial and others more analytical? What factors helped extend the conversation? What got in the way? Were certain ways of talking about race or racism more fruitful than others were?

When I interviewed students after classes, I discovered that the unfinished sentences and unanswered questions often prompted fresh thinking. In Chapter 4, I take up the ways in which students and teachers successfully worked to build a class culture where they could engage in serious conversations. I use examples from this chapter and other class conversations to explore the approaches that encouraged racial literacy.

4

Creating Opportunities to Talk
About Race and Racism

My next-door neighbor Kerry teaches communication studies at a local community college. His students are required to give five speeches a semester. He never assigns topics of race or racism, and his students—most of whom identify as Black and Latino—do not raise the topics. What would it take for Kerry to create opportunities to talk about these issues?

As the last chapter shows, students and teachers can and do talk about race and racism—with personal stories, anecdotes, and questions punctuating conversations. Lively as the class discussions were, however, students would not have broached the topics of race and racism had the teachers not encouraged the dialogue. The teachers structured the class to invite student involvement, explicitly putting the issues of race and racism on the table, making particular curricular decisions, asking questions, and modeling reflection. Their initiative encouraged the students in the class to speak out.

Kerry explained why he did not want to talk about race. "What if someone said something that made another student mad" he asked, "and the student went to my boss and told them that my class is racist? I could lose my job!"

"Yes," I agreed. "But what if you were able to set up the conditions in your class so that you could handle the fallout? People might say hurtful things, but you could manage the disagreement, and you could end up with students learning something important."

How did Ann and Lewis position their class for controversial discussions about race? How did they keep the conversations affable, if at times heated? What role did students play in extending conversations of race and racism—even for brief moments? To answer Kerry's questions, I draw on individual and small-group interviews conducted throughout the term to analyze several of the exchanges that took place in Lewis and Ann's class.

CLASS TONE AND STRUCTURE

Ann and Lewis worked to craft a trusting but challenging environment that supported students' critical reflection. The teachers actively encouraged students to participate. They explicitly taught students how to listen, back up their opinions with evidence, and make use of their own experiences in discussions. Students perceived conversations to be important because they related to the "real world." Making connections to personal experiences piqued students' curiosity and interest, and students participated actively.

Trust and Respect

The trusting atmosphere of the class took time to mold. Students needed to learn that they could trust the teachers. Lewis and Ann developed students' trust by taking them seriously. They challenged the students to be responsible for their words. Ann and Lewis responded to students' bigotry, sweeping generalizations, and statements they found hard to believe with questions, gentle warnings, and sometimes laughter. When students were attacking the special education program at a different school, for example, Ann couched a warning in a word of praise: "You guys are good about asking what do you mean and how do you know. But let's be careful before we make generalizations. Because we don't know [what is happening in that program]. Let's find out before we jump on it."

Lewis explained that it was important to both of them to encourage students' creativity, not stifle their motivation. "Ann's good at that," he explained, and reminded her of a time when she preserved a student's self-esteem: "You said, 'Well, I don't think that's particularly true.' Or 'Maybe . . .' instead of 'That's shit!' You didn't destroy [him]. I've seen the situation where the kids says 'Oh, God. I'm wrong again. I'm so stupid; I can't do this.'"

Lewis wanted the classroom to feel like a safe place emotionally as well as academically. As he stated in an interview, "I reinforce that my classroom is going to be safe, and you have the option to say how you feel." As is evident from the way several students described him, Lewis was often successful in his goal of making students feel comfortable. Tim described Lewis as a "regular guy." Similarly, Tricia described him as a teacher who gave positive reinforcement and did not hold himself above his students:

> He was comfortable being himself, [which] kind of like gave me the permission to be myself. And if I were to say something that deserved kudos, he would acknowledge it, and he'd be like, "Hey, you're a pretty smart girl" or whatever, you know? In class, I think that he tries to be the role model that kids our age need, you know? Somebody who's not going to be on their pedestal, looking down and saying, "This is what you need to do. I'm better than you."

In an interview, Lewis described how the trusting environment affected students' willingness to talk to each other: "A lot of it has to do with the atmosphere you set. If the atmosphere is a trusting one, people are more likely to release." Lewis saw students' respect for each other evolving throughout the year and explained that it was important for students to "talk instead of attacking people." Lewis gave the example of how Edmund, who used to be much more closed and superficial in discussions, began to listen to others and delve into serious conversations: "A perfect example is Edmund. . . . I just see him growing. . . . He's taken ownership in what's going on. . . . I think this is his third term with us. And he used to talk surface stuff. . . . Now he's getting to the meaning." Lewis described how Edmund contributed to the class by examining the statements and ideas of his classmates: "He's flipping [their comments] back over and looking at the picture for everybody. He says, 'I understand where you're coming from,' and he repeats what that person says and talks about it."

Both teachers facilitated discussions so that students were respectful of each other. Lewis worked to foster an orderly class environment. He tended to exert more control over class discussion than Ann did. Ann did share in the keeping of order, however. When students ganged up on another student, firing questions at her, for example, Ann reprimanded them: "You can ask that in different ways so that people don't feel like they are being attacked."

Challenge

While the tone of the class was trusting and respectful, the teachers at the same time challenged students to think critically. Ann and Lewis consistently pushed students to think broadly about difficult questions, and articulate and give evidence for their convictions. The language used in the journal questions reveals the critical nature of the teachers' approach. In "Who do you think should fight when your country is at war?" for example, Lewis did not say "our country" but rather "your country." By using the adjective "your" to describe country, he avoided a patriotic stance one might find in a U.S. history textbook. Rather, the teachers invited critical analysis by encouraging students to form their own opinions. By asking, "Who do you think . . .?" Lewis forcefully signaled that students' opinions were valued and that answers represented opinions, not facts. Instead of asking, "Who should fight . . .?"—which conceals the subjectivity of the answer—the question probed the idea of knowledge construction and made explicit the existence of bias in statements made in class.

The teachers structured activities so that they would challenge all students. Journal questions such as the one above gave all students a chance to gather their thoughts before being called on to speak. The teachers then gave each student a chance to share his or her answer with the class. Many students who tended not to speak up otherwise responded to these prompts.

While they asked challenging questions, Ann and Lewis also tried not to embarrass students. They often affirmed that mistakes were part of the learning process. Ann elaborated: "We also try to set it up from early on that we love to see people fail if it means that they're trying something. It's not really failing. If you're wrong about something, that's OK. At least we can try to figure out— If you got your facts wrong, we'll figure [it] out." When a student thought that *habitat* and *habitual* were from the same root, Ann simply asked, "Where's the dictionary?" Students looked up the word and read out the definitions. Understanding became a general question rather than a focus on an individual's mistake.

Ann and Lewis also encouraged students who were struggling. Lewis said he was most proud of one quiet student for "going from a seed to a flower and blooming." Ann relayed that she and Lewis had been told that another quiet student could not read. She proudly described the boy's accomplishments in the class, once they figured out materials that interested him.

There was definitely room for teachers to challenge students further. Nonetheless, I admired how the teachers were willing to take students seriously.

Seminar Format

In the beginning of the term, Ann introduced the idea of conducting seminars. She emphasized that students needed to listen to multiple points of view. Listening to the explanation, Sammy, a student, summarized the idea: "There's as many solutions [as there are people], well not necessarily solutions but beliefs."

The class discussion about seminars demonstrates the way the teachers and students listened, gave suggestions, and used humor and examples to try to convince each other:

> ANN: [A seminar is a] tried-and-true way. Lewis and I are not going to lead this. It's up to you to listen. . . . Do your best not to try to go over with the volume. (*She notices Philip.*) Yeah?
> PHILIP: This might sound childish, but I think it might actually work better if we started raising our hands.
> ANN: It might, but who would call on you if we don't have leaders?

Philip objected that in many discussions the person who gets the first word in is the one who gets to talk. Students joked about ways the class could overcome the problem:

> BILL: [We could use] buzzers.
> MJ: It's not like you can be in the middle of an argument and raise your hand and say, "Can I yell at you for a minute?"
> TRICIA: It's like a real-world discussion.
> ANN: What do you do if you don't have an actual one leader? It's every single person in the room's responsibility. It is everybody's job to lead. If you notice that someone is not talking, you can ask them. Some people participate just by being very good listeners. Ask questions. You guys are really good in here at asking questions. Rephrase. . . . The key is to listen.

Ann's explicit instruction, followed up by both teachers' reinforcement of the ideas in practice, helped create open and thoughtful discussions. In addition, students and teachers sat in a large square so they could all see each other when they talked. Such a class structure freed students to interact on a subject as potentially difficult as racism without being led every step of the way by a teacher. Having students of different races listen to each other was vital to everyone's learning, giving students tools for interaction outside the classroom, where there is not teacher guidance.

Like Tricia, who compared a seminar to "a real-world discussion," several students perceived both the seminar medium as well as the issues raised in class as meaningful and therefore important. Edmund characterized the subject matter of the class as "real issues that are facing us now" rather than "always talking about the slavery and being whipped." "Now that I have the chance to talk about the real issues," he added, "I *want* to!" Because he viewed discussion topics as important, Edmund wanted to be part of the conversation, even when it involved conflict: "Like that conversation [about police profiling] when Tim got mad, 'cause that's kind of a real issue."

EXPLICIT REFERENCES TO RACE AND RACISM

In many classes that are characterized by trust, respect, and intellectual challenge, the topic of race is still taboo or discussed only superficially. Although Ann and Lewis's class was a general U.S. History and Language Arts class, not one explicitly about race or racism, Ann and Lewis talked easily about race and racism. By doing so, they normalized to some extent what might have otherwise been a taboo topic. By talking personally about their racial positions in society, the teachers modeled the process of investigating the construction of race. In addition, they brought up topics that dealt explicitly with race, used materials that pointedly referred to racism, and racialized topics that could have been dealt with in a way that naturalized Whiteness or ignored racial factors.

Teachers Normalize Conversations About Race and Racism

The teachers made conversations about race ordinary. Lewis especially talked easily about race. In a discussion of the 1950s, for instance, Lewis described the racially charged reactions to Elvis Presley's music: "[Elvis] took Black music, so to speak, and he took that music and he introduced it on television. The *Ed Sullivan Show*. White southern Baptist preachers went crazy: 'There's this White man singing nigger music; he's going to drive our children to hell.'"

In addition, Lewis shared his personal experiences dealing with race. Lewis moved beyond the rhetoric of the civil rights movement, for instance, to bring the issue of segregation alive with a story about his hometown: "We had one Black pool in this small town, one public swimming pool. They closed that. We had to go back to swimming in the creek. Because they said 'The races will not mix.'"

He enjoyed telling students anecdotes, such as this one about how his mother had to pass a literacy test to be allowed to vote: "They made you pass a literacy test. And half of the people giving the literacy test didn't know what the hell it was in the first place. My mother went to vote, and they asked her to recite the Gettysburg Address. . . . But then she started off with the Constitution. The guy said, 'God, girl. You know what you talking about.' Hell, he didn't know either!"

Lewis laughed as he recalled the story. His easy laughter at his own experiences signaled his comfort with racial issues. bell hooks (2003) explains that humor can open conversations: "Humor is vital to our efforts to bond across race. Laughing together intervenes in our fear of making mistakes" (p. 63).

In an interview, Lewis said that he discussed his experiences so that students would "know where [he was] coming from." "I let them know that my attitude is shaped by who I am." Lewis explained to me that he also found a need to talk about race when others were blind to or neglected the issue. He said that he would call attention to race "purposely. To get them thinking."

Although she did not raise the issue as much as Lewis did, Ann, too, was comfortable with discussions of race. Introducing an assignment in which students were to research the progress of various groups since the 1950s, for example, Ann listed "Indians, Blacks, Hispanics, Asians, Whites, Gays and Lesbians, Disabled" on the chalkboard. She talked about how it is often difficult to figure out what language to use when referring to groups of people. "Do you say 'Black,' or do you say 'African American'?" she asked, and then explained that the night before she had seen George Carlin on television say that most Indians preferred the term *Indian* to the term *Native American*" Throughout the explanation, Ann seemed at ease exploring racial issues.

Teachers Examine Their Own Positions

The teachers were also willing to examine their own positions. Modeling personal reflection opened the door to conversations about race and racism. In one conversation, Ann's reflection on the exclusiveness of her language led to a brief conversation that interrogated the construction of race. Ann had used the pronoun *we* to describe the Europeans who had taken or purchased land in the Midwest in the 1800s. She laughed after she spoke, realizing that she had unconsciously identified everyone in the class with White Europeans. In an interview later, Ann explained: "It was because I was looking around at all the Black kids and started saying *we*, and thought 'Gosh!' And I said, 'Wait a minute. You weren't one of the *we*'s. You didn't go across the— you know, take Nebraska away from the Indians.'"

After she laughed, Ann corrected herself; and in response, three students referred to their own ancestry, which was different from that of

White Europeans. They tacitly agreed with Ann's self-correction, calling into question the accuracy of an inclusive *we*:

> Ann: When I say *we*, I mean White Europeans.
> Antoine: (*under his breath*) I was going to say!
> Vic: We came over to build the railroad.
> Cliff: To tell you the truth, I don't know when I came over.

Students connected themselves to racial groups from the past. (Vic, for instance, had been born in Korea and adopted by White parents; he identified with Asian immigrant railroad workers of the previous century.) In doing so, they posed a question of racial identity—Who am I?—and challenged the way that race is often constructed, indicating that being White is not a universal experience.

Ann considered her students' racial identities and interrogated her own White privilege. Modeling reflection, Ann opened the door for students to challenge the norm of Whiteness. It was striking that these students voiced their beliefs and challenges aloud.

Moments of reflection tended to be short lived. In this case, right after the brief glance at identity and racial construction, some students expressed violent and stereotypical attitudes toward American Indians:

> Ann: Imagine that you settled in Nebraska, and the Dakota Sioux
>   [fought to keep their land].
> Jake: We stomp on them.
> Edmund: I'll fight with [alongside] the Indians, Goddamn it. For real.
> Vic: . . . I don't want to get scalped.

Reflecting on one aspect of racism (universalizing Whiteness) did not prevent students from trivializing and stereotyping, in this case the encounter between Whites and Native Americans. Nonetheless, Ann's thinking aloud opened the door to conversations about race and racism.

Both Ann and Lewis were aware of issues of race, racism, oppression, and privilege. They thought about how race and racism worked in their own lives. In an interview, for example, Ann discussed her complicity in a racist society. She also realized how much more work she herself has to do to counteract her own tendencies:

> I learn something [about racism] every day. I get a new awareness of that every day. I don't think that's something that [I have completely figured out]. . . . Because, you know, I am quite aware

that I'm part of a racist society. I've got my own racist kinds of reactions to things. I know I do!

Ann continually tried to learn more about racial and other forms of oppression. She was particularly interested in issues of socioeconomic status, women's rights, and Native American land rights. She kept an eye out for articles and artifacts. She told me, for instance, about a bumper sticker that graphically showed in overlaid maps how the American state of Nebraska is actually, by treaty, Indian territory. "There's this one wonderful bumper sticker you can get that shows Nebraska, and the Indian Territory just covering the entire place, 'cause that is the treaty. [The treaty is] still in effect."

In this class, then, the teachers were comfortable raising issues of race and racism with their students. They knew and continued to learn about experiences and histories of people and groups, and they thought these topics were important to talk about with students. They used their own positions and experiences, including those related to their race, to enrich conversations about race and racism. In addition, as the next section shows, the teachers assigned readings specifically about race and racism.

A Particularly Provocative Text

Ann and Lewis provided provocative materials (videos, statistics, newspaper editorials and other readings) to stimulate discussions about race and racism. These discussions often snowballed, accumulating a variety of ideas and applications. As you saw in Chapter 3, the poem by Cervantes (1990) particularly stirred the students and teachers. This poem elicited anger and humor. The discussion evoked students' and teachers' curiosity about racism. It allowed them to question and identify with the oppression described in the poem.

Philip, for example, articulated and investigated his perceptions of racism. When he began speaking, he argued that Whites who did not understand their own racism would benefit from reading the poem. As he went on, however, he wrestled with the difficulty Whites might have in comprehending racism. He recognized that Whites often made excuses for accounts of racism, but he was not sure how one might go about convincing them: "They need to read *this* poem. And then once they read it, they'll probably just say, "Oh, that's just another minority complaining but—." Although Philip did not come up with an answer that was satisfying to him, the poem served as a catalyst for his critical questioning.

The poem also generated personal discussion of racism. It empowered students to speak forcefully about the existence of racism, which was notable, particularly because students in the class often questioned or denied the existence of racism today, preferring to portray racism as a thing of the past. Edmund explained that the poem was significant: "These two little lines, they just said a lot to me."

Edmund's passionate argument for the existence of racism and his condemnation of his own friends for pretending racism did not exist or did not matter was one of the most striking examples of engagement of the whole term. Although he seemed to capitulate in the face of Leslie's objections ("I didn't do anything to you"), Edmund later went on to describe the personally painful effects of racism. Using the language of the poem, he explained: "Some of the things that happened to me because of it, like scars, intellectual scars, inside, not like on the body, you know, I can't reason them away." He also used the poem as evidence that Lewis was justified in calling attention to race and racism.

Not only did the poem bring about strong responses from students, but these responses in turn provoked teachers to introduce more material that spurred student discussion. Ann described a photograph that evoked powerful emotional responses: "There's a picture of a little kid whose grandfather is in the Ku Klux Klan—it's a little White kid. And the grandfather is helping the child sort of adjust his robe. He's got a little tiny Ku Klux Klan robe on." Her description of the image sparked a debate about whether or not it is child abuse to teach your child to be racist. Although she did not use the phrase *institutionalized oppression*, Ann's representation of a family's perpetuation of racism was a powerful example of the concept.

STUDENTS' UNSPOKEN REACTIONS

Lively discussions prompted students' thinking about racism, even when they did not speak out in class. As a result of the discussion of the KKK photograph, Leslie thought about how one learns racism from one's parents. After class she remarked, "I never thought about it like that before," in reference to the idea that teaching children racism might be child abuse. She then made a connection to her own life: that her friend's boyfriend had learned racism from his father.

In interviews after the class, students recalled the discussion of the poem as important. Leslie quoted the same lines that Edmund had quoted during the discussion:

LESLIE: I liked the part when it said "you think that—" I don't remember exactly, but, "you think I'm crazy 'cause I think there's snipers hiding in the locker room," or something. . . . But then, it was just like, "they're not shooting at you." And so it's like I kind of got that maybe I can't talk about racism because I'm not Black and I wouldn't know. So, kind of like that. I was like, "Well, maybe there's more than I think there is." But I think that I would notice.

JB: That's interesting that you don't see them, so it made you realize that maybe there's things that you aren't seeing.

LESLIE: Yeah. I mean, I don't think that there's much racism around, but I'm not the one who's getting discriminated against.

Leslie went back and forth in trying to understand that racism might exist even if she didn't see it. She interrogated her beliefs ("Maybe there's more [racism] than I think there is"), but then immediately expressed doubt about the new idea and summoned evidence against it ("But I think that I would notice"). If only for a brief moment, however, the poem and Edmund's comment prompted Leslie to step outside her usual perspective (one in which she denounced Lewis as a "whiny bitch" because she thought he complained about racism too much) and think about racism in a new light.

A conversation I had with another student, Chris, after class one day also demonstrates the way in which students, even when quiet during class, made connections between what was happening in the discussion and other issues. Chris had mentioned segregation when the class was talking about gays in the military. In an interview, I asked him what he meant by the comment. He explained that Vic, advocating for separate showers for people who are gay, made him think of a story his father told him:

JB: Today we were in the middle of talking about gays in the military, and you just all of a sudden said, "That would be segregation." I didn't know what you were thinking when you said that. . . .

CHRIS: I just figured that's segregation. I didn't know if it was or wasn't. I just said it 'cause it seemed like that.

JB: And do you think it is?

CHRIS: Well, what Vic said about having different showers, yeah. 'cause I remember my dad telling me stories about when he was in high school, that . . . his friend Bobby Peterson would go into the Black shower with a sock with like a bar of soap in

> there, you know. . . . And he just remembers his friend Bobby
> Peterson didn't like Black people.
> JB: And what did he tell you about that?
> Chris: That Bobby Peterson would walk into the Black shower with
> a sock and start whippin' on people, ya know.

Class discussion was a vehicle for Chris to connect discrimination against gays to discrimination against Blacks. Even when students do not articulate their reflections, class discussions help them make associations that they otherwise might not make. Bringing up controversial "real-world" topics ensured that students had had at least a possibility of making these connections. Along with raising controversial topics, teachers used questions to plant seeds that promoted critical thinking.

TEACHERS USE QUESTIONS

Ann and Lewis often asked provocative questions that prompted discussion of racism. Many classes started with a question to get students thinking and writing about the topic of the day. These journal questions invited students' critical reflection, especially as Lewis and Ann emphasized the need to support one's opinions with evidence. During class discussions, Ann and Lewis also used follow-up questions to push students to explore the nature of race and racism.

One example of a teacher questioning was during the discussion of the poem. Philip talked about how difficult it is for White people who have not had much contact with Blacks to understand that Blacks do not have equal rights. In order to help the class think about how people's perceptions change, Ann followed Philip's comment with a question: "How long are the White people going to be in authority in America?" Her question led several students to talk about the effect of changing racial demographics in the United States. It would have been helpful to investigate a few of the ideas more thoroughly, but the question itself had been a good start.

In a discussion about prisoners, teachers used questions to highlight the ways in which race affects how people are likely to be treated. When the students were suggesting sending criminals to war, Lewis called attention explicitly to the racial makeup of prisons: "Who is the biggest majority of people in [this state's] prisons?"

Continuing in the same vein, Ann asked about the Vietnam War, a reference to the fact that a disproportionate number of Blacks fought in the war: "Who fought in the Vietnam War?" Lewis then asked Tim to look at the institutionalized racism that might have caused disproportionate numbers of African Americans to be imprisoned. He followed up his own question by giving an example of his experience with the police and asking whether a White teacher would have faced the same treatment. While the pace was quick and not everyone participated, this discussion resulted in at least some students examining and articulating their views and acknowledging at least the possibility of institutionalized racism. Even when the teachers' questions were not answered directly, they nonetheless guided the discussion in critical directions.

Another powerful example of questioning occurred when the class discussed the U.S. military involvement in Kosovo. Both teachers asked questions that allowed students to see the war through the lens of race. Ann asked students why the United States was fighting in Kosovo but did not address similar levels of conflict in areas of Africa. Her question was neither detached nor academic; rather, her tone suggested her genuine concern and curiosity about the discrepancies between military policies in Europe, which has a predominantly White population, and Africa, which is predominantly Black:

> There are a lot of wars and killing going on . . . in Africa. Are we bombing them? Are we worried? I was told by the people who got us in to this war [in Kosovo] that the purpose is to stop the killing.

Here, Ann was not trying to address all the complexity of military decisionmaking. Rather, she chose to focus on one racial question.

Lewis asked an even bolder question, pointing to the racial element of the U.S. response: "Could it be that if you're White, you're right?" Discussing the topic in a small-group interview afterwards, Tricia said that the idea that military policy would have to do with race surprised her: "When [Lewis] brought the color into it . . . that totally threw me off, 'cause I wasn't thinkin' it had anything to do with that." Realizing that the military might perpetuate institutionalized racism was a new awareness for Tricia.

Questions helped students think about the institutionalized racism in the society around them. When the class was talking about a collage of famous Americans of the 1950s, for example, Ann got students to think about the unacknowledged contributions made by people of color: "Where did Elvis [Presley] get his music?" Two students responded to the question:

Vic: African music.
Antoine: Rhythm and blues.

In the same discussion, I asked whether Edmund Hillary, the man recognized in the image as being the first to climb Mount Everest, was really the first person to do so. Vic suggested that "the people who lived around there" probably had climbed it.

"Maybe he was the first White man who went up," Mike suggested quietly. "The first man who got credit for it."

Although there was no extended discussion about the African or African American influences on Presley's music or the other possible Mount Everest climbers, the questions served to expand the conversation into the realm of race.

TEACHERS ENCOURAGE STUDENTS' QUESTIONS

Not only did teachers ask questions; they also encouraged students' questions and comments, explicitly supporting students' risk taking. Students' outspoken stances were an important factor in initiating and extending discussions about racism. How did teachers foster students' outspokenness? One way was by explicitly modeling and giving students the language to question each other. "What do you mean?" and "How do you know?" required that students deal with more than just superficial knowledge.

One day at the beginning of the term, Hank asked, "Would the government hide the existence of UFOs?"

Ann interceded loudly: "Wait, wait, wait, wait! What do you mean by the government?" After a few comments, she stepped in again: "One of the things you need to do in this class is always ask, 'What do you mean and how do you know?' When you say 'the government,' you have to back up what you say."

Then Lewis instructed students to "put on the inside of your folder: 'What do you mean and how do you know it?'" He wanted the students to see those questions every time they opened their folders.

Furthermore, when a problem or issue came up during class that students could not answer adequately, the teachers told them to write the question in a special place in the back of their notebooks. When the students tried to go back to arguing about UFOs, Ann interrupted, "Wait. You are not going to convince each other. Write down the question."

Not reaching closure can be uncomfortable for students. When students wondered why they should write down the questions, Tim interpreted Ann's direction. "We can't answer the question," he explained to his classmates. "You just gotta ask it."

Ann explained why she thought the questions were important: "Let's get the questions down; as the term goes on, we'll get some information down. Maybe we'll never know. That's what a democracy is all about. So what is the question?" The class was silent. "Everyone has answers but no one has questions?" she asked with a smile.

Later in the class period, Ann and Lewis explained to the class why they thought it important to write down questions:

> ANN: I'm going to explain myself about why [we're] stopping for questions. When you get really involved in something, once you write the questions down, we don't want to let them go. When you come to the end of the term we'll have a better understanding of the questions.
> LEWIS: We run across something and we ask what happened to it.
> ANN: It's good to get passionate about something.

By valuing passion, Ann was giving students permission to have strong feelings and ideas and to wonder about them openly.

In addition to encouraging students to ask respectful, clarifying, authentic questions during discussion, the teachers used students' questions in their assessments. When they were finishing their unit on the 1960s, for example, Ann handed each student three index cards and asked them to write a good question on each card with the answer on the back. She explained that some answers would be hard to fit on the back of a card but that students should write the beginning of an answer. The next day she organized the cards and used many of the students' questions for a quiz about the unit.

It is impossible to tell how directly the teachers' encouragement prompted the students' questioning in class, but the ongoing support for students' questions clearly affected discussions. On the first day of the term, when students were introducing themselves and saying why they had returned to the class, Philip voiced his appreciation of the atmosphere that Ann and Lewis had created: "I like the way we can learn." Philip's curiosity was encouraged and supported by the teachers in the class. In the discussion of the poem, he responded to Steve's simple but persistent request for input: "Anybody else want to add anything about the poem? Final statements? Things that they liked about it? Things that they didn't understand about it?"

Later, when Jake jokingly chided him for stereotyping, Ann explicitly requested that students allow Philip to continue: "Let him finish." With Ann's support, Philip did continue exploring the subject. Teachers can prompt students' reflection by asking questions, as seen above, but students can also be instrumental in initiating discussions when speaking out is sanctioned.

STUDENTS NOTICE AND RESPOND TO RACIAL ISSUES

Teachers convey their trust in students when they allow them to talk about issues that matter to them. In Lewis and Ann's class, students' input and their willingness to speak out were important factors in the dialogues built by the class.

Reflectiveness

Personal reflection buoyed the extent to which students noticed and responded to racial issues in class: Students who had reflected on racism more deeply were more likely to extend conversations about racism than those who had not thought about the issue as much. In many cases Black, Asian, and racially mixed students were more vocal and articulate about race and racism than White students, but a student's race alone did not determine whether or not he or she contributed to critical discussions about race and racism. Rather, students' interest in and reflection on the racial significance of their experiences as well as their willingness to speak out in the context of the class were key to their involvement in discussions.

At the beginning of the term, some students questioned Whiteness being privileged. When the class was looking at a collage depicting people and events from the 1950s, Antoine, a Black student, asked outright: "How come there ain't no colored folks in here?" He repeated the observation, and Vic, who is Asian, echoed the idea: "Ain't no Asian people."

In the same discussion of the 1950s, someone described Elvis Presley as the "King of Rock." Cliff, who identified as mixed Black and White, objected to the classification. "Man! Run DMC [a Black musician] is the King of Rock," he interjected. Antoine's, Vic's, and Cliff's comments called into question the ways the class was considering people of color.

All students have experiences in which their race matters, but Antoine, Vic, and Cliff were more aware of the racial implications of their experiences than many of the White students in the class. Most of the students of color in the class with whom I spoke described experiences in which their race mattered. Edmund, for example, talked about a time when someone told him a racist joke on the phone, and Vic described a time as a child when neighborhood boys would not let him play basketball because he was Asian. Similarly, Cliff was pained by the derogatory racial remarks he often heard from both the Black and White sides of his family.

From individual and small-group interviews, I found that most of the White students had not thought much about race or racism, other than to tout colorblindness. If they did identify as White, they did not think such identification had any meaning or significance. As McIntosh (1988) and others (Kincheloe & Steinberg, 1998; McIntyre, 1997) have described, Whites often do not think of themselves as having a race, and this was the case for many of the White students.

In an interview, Tim bemoaned the fact that it seemed that "Black people think that you're against them just 'cause you're White" without connecting this perception to any institutional aspect of racism. In fact, he did not think there was anything, other than some undefined "technicalities," that made being White significant or privileged:

> I don't think [being White is] like anything. I just think it's like being a person, is how I look at it. I'm a person. I'm not White. I'm beige. I'm Caucasian. What's it like? I think there's certain things, like, technicalities, and it's going to be different being a Black person. Or Asian or Mexican or whatever.

Similarly, at times, Hank read his own race as little more than skin color. When asked, he only obliquely contemplated what it meant to be White: He turned the question around and wondered what it would be like to be of another race, as if one only experienced race if one were not White:

> HANK: With me, everybody in my family is White. I got the blond hair . . . and my skin's kind of real light. . . . That's just how people see me, just being White. You're just "White boy." You know. Nothin' to you.
>
> JB: What do you mean, "Nothin' to you"?
>
> HANK: There's nothin' in you but White or . . . German . . . but I'm sure there's a whole bunch of stuff along the line.
>
> JB: What do you think of being White?
>
> HANK: What do I think of being White? How do you mean?
>
> JB: Well, I don't know. Do you think about it much?
>
> HANK: (*long pause*) I wonder some . . . I don't know about the question, but I wonder sometimes, like, what it would be like if I was Black, or if I was a certain other race.

At the same time that he seemed to dismiss the significance of being White in this interview, Hank, who had grown up playing with Black children

("I lived up in those projects up there," he said in an interview, pointing out the window; "I was the only White kid around"), did mention and question the significance of race a few times in class discussions. For instance, he argued that Blacks were more likely to get stopped by police than Whites were. Hank's experiences living around Blacks may have made him more likely to see his own Whiteness at times and recognize certain aspects of racial oppression.

Hank's not talking about race when I asked him directly, but talking about race in class, may illustrate the fact that concrete discussions can be more powerful than those that are abstract. Hank was less articulate with me in formal interviews than he was in off-the-cuff-remarks in class. "What does it mean to be White?" may be a much less useful question for discussion than "Do you think Blacks get stopped by the police more in your neighborhood than Whites?"

Curiosity

Curiosity also influenced students' involvement in discussions of race. Prompted by Tabitha's "mulatto" comment, Hank, who was sitting next to me, leaned over and asked me, "Isn't there a possibility that there was a Black man in my family?" In an interview, he explained that he and Antoine had discussed race that day in a side conversation about skin color. "It just got me thinking," he said, "of like, like when you see people come from other countries or whatever, that are African or whatever, that are really Black, you know charcoal Black, kind of like—." He said the adjectives with an embarrassed smile in his voice. "And, uh, I looked at [Edmund] and Antoine, and I said, 'The color of your skin looks like you guys had, generations ago, had like some White people in your family along the line.' You know, and maybe I had some, a Black person in my family along the line a couple hundreds of years ago or something like [that]; and we were just talking like that."

Hank was attaining insight into the profound racial heritage of the United States:

> This kid I know up the street, he's White, you know, and his great grandma is Black. And it just got me thinking. . . . Oh, and then I said . . . if the world lasts a thousand years or two thousand years, the majority of people in the United States are probably going to be colored, you know? Because of all the interracial relationships— Like Black and White, because the baby comes out (*pause*) dark,

you know like colored. It is considered colored. . . . People don't think about that. You only think about your mom, your grandma, and your great-grandma. That's about it.

The comments reveal how curious White students can be about issues of race and identity. Tricia, Tim, Chris, Richard, and even Leslie expressed interest in talking about race, but they did so primarily outside class in individual interviews.

Philip was a White student who had some awareness of the influence of racism and was curious to know more. Interested in the meaning of the word *Oriental*, Philip was the only White student who participated actively in the exchange about the terms *mulatto* and *Oriental* during the discussion of the poem. Unlike some of the other White students, Philip, I discovered in interviews, was quite cognizant of racial issues. This consciousness, as well as, in this case, his curiosity, prompted him to participate in discussions of race and racism.

Students' participation in discussions of race and racism, then, is related to but not dependent on students' race. It is not necessary to have a group that identifies as racially mixed in order to discuss race and racism. Neither are racial differences a sufficient factor alone in discussion.

CONCLUSION

Ann and Lewis struggled over how to create this class. What kinds of questions should we ask? What materials and assignments should we use? How can we best cultivate trust and encourage discussion? How do we structure the physical environment? How much should we allow students to guide discussion? Will they get it? At the end of the term, Ann looked back and said, "Sometimes I feel like [we] just totally bomb, and other times I think it works."

Discussions about race and racism in Lewis and Ann's class were often lively. Even before 9:00 A.M., students in blue jeans and baseball hats would be leaning forward, keen to follow the exchanges. Many students contributed to the discussions. This was not an honors class, but a class of teenagers at risk of dropping out of high school. How did the engagement happen?

Although outspoken stances factored into students' engagement in conversations about race and racism, that alone was not enough. Neither did interest in the topics guarantee participation. While outspokenness, reflection, and curiosity helped extend discussions, students required direction in order to engage in discussions of race and racism in the first place.

Direction in this class took the form of teacher questions and provocative curricular materials presented in an atmosphere and format that invited participation. Provided, as they were, with material as compelling as Cervantes' poem, for instance, and provocative questions, students responded with meaningful debate. Sometimes the class engaged topics only briefly, but at least the conversations were started, and, contrary to the concern of my neighbor Kerry, they stayed within reasonable bounds.

One way in which Ann and Lewis maintained a respectful atmosphere in the class was by using and teaching students to use two powerful questions. "What do you mean?" and "How do you know?" are disarming questions; I have even used them with strangers. In a coffee shop, a White woman struck up a conversation with me about what she called the "reverse racism" in the poor Latino and Black community in which she worked. Although I believe that anyone can discriminate, I think that to be considered racist one has to have the social or economic power to enforce one's prejudice. I knew, however, that it would do little good to launch into a tirade about institutionalized racism and classism. It also dawned on me that I was jumping to conclusions about what she meant by "reverse racism." I decided to ask her, "What do you mean by reverse racism?" Without being confrontational, the simple question forced the woman to articulate her own power in the situation and rethink her blaming stance.

Using all different kinds of kindling, teachers sparked classroom discussions, and students were drawn to the fire. I was with them for only 12 weeks, which is very little time to observe the subtle changes that I believe were occurring. On some days, students were tired; on other days, they were distracted. However, even students who were not particularly outgoing, knowledgeable, or articulate responded to many of the class's discussions of race and racism. In a class where they had learned to trust their teachers, ask questions, and express their opinions, students engaged in meaningful discussions of racism. The class succeeded in having students rethink their assumptions "just by bringing up subjects like [racism] and letting us argue 'em out," Tim explained during an interview. "I don't think [Lewis] makes me a better person or whatever," he continued. "He just makes me think about things a little bit different."

By encouraging active and critical student engagement in issues of race and racism, this class succeeded in opening students' eyes to new ways of thinking. Having these discussions, however, was not always easy. Students sometimes narrowly characterized race and racism. The next chapter analyzes class discussions to understand the ways in which students made meanings and how teachers can broaden definitions.

5

Characterizations of Race and Racism

Lewis and Ann were experienced teachers who cultivated a class that was playful and respectful and a place where students and teachers seriously examined racial issues. In several conversations, however, the class seemed to skirt the political and institutional aspects of race and racism. Echoing ideas and opinions that they heard at home, among friends, in the media and popular culture, and at school, students often characterized race as natural or trivial. They often described racism as a thing of the past or as personal or extreme, rather than institutional.

At the same time, students resisted these cultural messages. They could question generalizations and stereotypes. Students' words and actions are not barriers to discussions but building blocks, the very materials that teachers have to work with to develop students' racial literacy. This chapter explores the ways that students characterized race and racism and ways that teachers can challenge those characterizations. Given what students bring to the classroom, what would enable us to deepen conversations?

CHARACTERIZATIONS OF RACE

Earlier, I suggested that it is beneficial to understand race as socially constructed. Students in Lewis and Ann's class needed help to do this. They often did the opposite, characterizing race as a natural or essential phenomenon. They also minimized the importance of race, advocating colorblindness. Both essentializing and colorblindness are dangerous because they can shut down conversations. How do we identify instances of essentializing and colorblindness? And, once we have identified them, how do we steer around these potential dead ends?

Essentializing Race

To essentialize race is to portray it as a predetermined and deterministic aspect of personality or life, as opposed to a social and historical construction that is constantly shifting. If I essentialize, then I imply that race is a fundamental and absolute category that means something concrete. Phrases such as *acting White* or *Black English*, for instance, convey the idea that certain ways of being are entirely contingent on membership in a racial group. People are often judged against an essential norm, such as being "not Chinese enough" or "too light skinned." Essentializing is in many ways like stereotyping: It involves generalizing about what it means to be of a certain race. We all essentialize. The trick is not to let essentializing put an end to a conversation.

In one statement, Edmund characterized the experience of being Black as essentially different from being White: "I can see from this poem you'll never understand. A young White man will never understand . . . what it's like to be a young Black man." His comment implied that being Black has a specific meaning and that Whites will never understand that meaning.

In an interview after the class, Tim discussed his assumption that he was different from a Black person and could not understand what it would be like to be Black. He referred to Edmund's implication that Blackness is essentially different from Whiteness: "There's certain things that I'll never understand. Like Edmund was saying earlier. A young White person will never know what it's like to be a young Black person."

Because the class had not examined race as a social construction, Tim was not able to engage in what may have been a productive discussion about racism. Instead, he was afraid of offending his Black classmates and teacher. Tim described his fear—based on the assumption of difference—of talking about issues of race and racism.

> I feel like I gotta be careful 'cause if I say something a little bit sensitive about the race thing then [Lewis and Edmund will] just be like, "No. You don't understand! You're White, you don't . . ." you know? So, I think I guard about what I say. Because there's not really an argument that I could put up if they were to say something like that. "You don't know. How are you supposed to know? Look at you; you're White!"

Although he seemed to be willing to participate in a dialogue about difference, Tim's fear escalated. His assumption that he could not understand led to frustration and anger.

What am I gonna say? I am White. I *don't* know what it's like to be Black. I can just think about it, and I can just tell you what I, as a White person, think. . . . Well, man, a young Black person will never know what it's like to be a young White person, either. Why do you gotta say shit like that? A young Black person will never know what it's like to have Black people think that you're against them just 'cause you're White. You'll never know what that feels like.

By saying that another person will never know what something feels like, Tim implied that there is no use trying to describe the feeling or find common ground. The progression from essentializing to fear to anger left little room for discussion.

Tim was a tall senior who spoke in confident tones a great deal in the class. His admission that he was intimidated indicated the powerful effect of essentializing race. It is important that we acknowledge students' caution about essentializing but at the same time help them study the institutional forces that lump people into groups based on perceived race. Asking questions about what makes a person a member of a racial group can disarm the loaded topic of race. Students might examine the "one-drop rule" (the idea that a person is Black if any of his or her ancestors was Black) and other laws and social practices that determine the categories they see as natural or unchanging.

I know from conversations with Edmund that he understood that larger institutional forces shaped the lives of Blacks and Whites and therefore some of the reasons their lives were different. However, his statement in class gave little indication that social forces make a difference in people's experiences. A mitigating explanation or question might have come from a teacher. Lewis and Ann were good at asking, "What do you mean and how do you know?" They might have asked those questions in this instance. "How do you know that a young White man will never understand what it is like to be a young Black man?" To diffuse the absoluteness—or prioritization—of race as a category, they might have said, "What factors other than our race impact our experience of the world?" or "Why was the poem titled 'For the Young White Man' if it is true that a White person cannot understand what it is like to be of a different race? The title implies that Cervantes wanted to open the discussion about racism." Another possible question would be, "What would Cervantes have said about Edmund's statement? Can you cite specific lines from the poem to provide evidence for your answers?"

Rather than seeing essentializing as a strictly negative impulse, we can use it to challenge stereotypes. Students who seem sure about what it means to be of another race can see the problem of essentializing when teachers ask them to define what it means to be of their race. Educator Alice McIntyre (2003) has her White students make a collage showing what it means to be White using words and images from magazines. They soon realize that one might contest *any* meaning attached to race. Similarly, in an elementary school in New York City where Latino students described Whites as "beasting," "greedy," and "rich," I asked students to describe what it meant to be Dominican and Puerto Rican. Students' difficulty in describing themselves as well as their lack of consensus demonstrated how fragile their definitions are.

Unless we challenge students when they essentialize, conversations can become polarized and paralyzed. An equally paralyzing effect can happen if students do the opposite of essentializing: when they only talk about people as individuals or portray themselves as "colorblind."

Colorblindness

Almost at an opposite extreme from essentializing, colorblindness dismisses the significance and relevance of race. In the class, students often talked as if they were colorblind, that is, as if race had no significance. Patricia Williams (1997a) described an example of the painful irony—and impossibility—of colorblindness and the other ways in which some people try to ignore significant aspects of identity:

> Someone has just announced in no uncertain terms that he or she hates you because you're dark, let's say, or Catholic or a woman or the wrong height, and the panicked authority figure tries to patch things up by reassuring you that race or gender or stature or your heartfelt religion doesn't matter; means nothing in the calculation of your humanity; is the most insignificant little puddle of beans in the world. (p. 4)

Williams pointed out that maintaining colorblindness is inherently contradictory in our culture: "How precisely does the issue of color remain so powerfully determinative of everything from life circumstance to manner of death, in a world that is, by and large, officially 'color-blind'?" (1997a, p. 15).

Tabitha's statement during one class discussion, "It doesn't matter what color you are," is a good example of colorblindness. Tabitha wanted to avoid exacerbating differences: "It doesn't matter what color you are, there's someone out there [who can hear you]." Similarly, Tricia, another White student, was vehement about not wanting to pigeonhole people.

"I don't really label kids," she remarked in an interview. "Labels are for cans."

Professions of colorblindness are inherently self-contradicting. As educator Christine Sleeter (1993) pointed out, "People do not deny seeing what they actually do not see. Rather they profess to be color-blind when trying to suppress negative images they attach to people of color" (p. 161). In an interview, Tim explained that although he had racial stereotypes, he tried to ignore them because those negative images would get in the way of his becoming friends with others:

> I just see it as—or I *try* to as much as I can—to see it as a person. Everybody has their stereotypes. . . . But, . . . like I said, I try to keep it as human as possible, instead of color. Because if I based people on their color, then there's a lot of good friends that I wouldn't have that I do have now. So I try not to base it like that. 'Cause I think it'd be cool to hang out with Edmund. He's nice. He's *smart*! . . . I'd like to kick it with him. And, like, oh, by the way he's Black (*mocking*). Who cares?! . . . There are people I like and I don't like, but I don't— I try not to base it on color.

In other interviews, Tim showed cognizance of ways in which race affects him, but he continually explained that he did his best to overlook his prejudice.

Although less often than many of their White peers, some Black and Chicano students also downplayed the significance of race. In a small-group interview, one of the students wanted everyone to identify himself by race. Mike (whom his friends called by his last name, Flores) only wanted to be known by his name. He did not identify himself as Chicano until pushed to do so, and when he did, he seemed unsure of the meaning of the term:

> MIKE: What do I call myself?
> STUDENT: Flores.
> MIKE: Nnnn, just me. Pretty much that's it.
> EDMUND: Flores.
> MIKE: I don't know. I don't call myself nothin'. I just chill.
> JB: But when I said "kids of color" you put yourself in that
>   category?
> MIKE: Uh, put myself in that category? I don't know. Where I'm
>   from, Dallas, everybody calls them Chicanos. That's, what do

you call it? Mexicans, light-skinned Mexicans, got White in 'em. I guess that's it.

During this conversation about racial identification, Edmund, Antoine, and Mike explained that race did not matter much. I asked if they ever talked about race explicitly. They responded:

EDMUND: Not really.
ANTOINE: Not really. It's not really a big issue. Not any more.
MIKE: (*overlapping*) We don't really care. It don't matter what color you is.

These students claimed that race was "not really a big issue." Yet earlier in the conversation, Edmund had reacted to Cliff's uses of the words *half-breed* and *mulatto*:

EDMUND: I don't like the word *mulatto*
JB: Why not?
EDMUND: 'Cause it's like a mule. A horse and a donkey reproduce and they have a mule, and it can't reproduce. It's a degrading word.

The language of race was clearly important, at least to Edmund. The apparent discrepancy between students' denial of its importance and their immediate reactions underscores students' uncertain and shifting positions with regard to colorblindness.

It is not clear to me to what extent the social context influenced students downplaying the importance of race. Mike was the only Chicano in the group; he might have minimized his racial identification because he did not want call attention to that difference or have to explain himself to others. In addition, my presence as a White person and the setting of the majority-White school might have influenced some students in the group (all of whom identified as Black, mixed, Asian. or Chicano) to downplay the importance of race.

If students had learned more about the historical construction of race, would they still hold on to the idea that race does not matter? Would they differentiate between race as a factor that affects personal interactions, and race as an element that is relevant at the level of institutions?

WHAT CAN WE DO ABOUT COLORBLINDNESS AND ESSENTIALIZING?

There are several ways to address colorblindness and essentializing.

- Given students' positive tendencies not to want to be prejudiced, it is helpful to assure students that we are not judging them and to encourage students not to be judgmental of each other. Everything a student says is an opportunity to grow. A teacher might have reassured Tabitha that she probably did not mean to offend anyone but at the same time urged the class to look at the larger historical and social forces that have led to the use of loaded words such as *Oriental* and *mulatto*.
- If students blame themselves or others in ways that get in the way of respectful discussion, depersonalizing the questions can help them examine a broader range of emotions and explanations. Explicitly differentiating personal prejudice from institutionalized racism also allows students to feel less personal guilt. We can offer a variety of sources of evidence of institutional factors. Students who realize that institutions perpetuate racism can approach the question without blaming themselves and therefore be less defensive.
- It can be helpful for teachers to request that students suspend their disbelief. "For the sake of argument, let's suppose that it is true that the color of one's skin makes a difference in people's lives." They can then ask students to explore evidence they might have otherwise ignored.
- Sometimes it's easier to understand racism when we look at parallels with oppressions that we already recognize. I might counter claims of colorblindness by explaining that I used to think there was no sexism in this country until I read that in heterosexual couples where both spouses have full-time jobs, women do significantly more of the housekeeping and child rearing. Of course, this kind of example can open another can of worms, but it is one way to break the silence that can come as a result of expressions of colorblindness. We can normalize racism by situating it in a group of oppressions, some of which may be less loaded for students. We must be careful, however, not to marginalize race.
- When students are essentializing, they often state or imply assumptions quickly. We may need at these times to slow the conversation down. One of the best ways is do so is to simply state

a reaction or feeling. For instance, a teacher can remark that a comment seems like a dead end. "I'm not sure where we can go with that. Is there another way to look at this that allows us to find some options?" or "If I won't ever understand what it means to be [a certain race], is there anything else I can do?"

- Another way to slow the conversation down is to articulate dilemmas so that students can see specific contradictions or complications. Educator Ira Baumgarten (personal communication, Dec. 11, 2003) uses the formula "How can we _____ while at the same time ____?" to deal with all sorts of controversial issues. In this case, teachers might ask, "How can we talk about racism while at the same time acknowledging that it might be difficult or even impossible for people to know what it is like to be of a different race?" By naming some known coordinates, we can more easily find our way into understanding rather than getting lost in speedy assumptions.

- In discussions where students are actively vying for the floor, it is common to let stereotypes pass unchallenged. While we could never carry on a conversation if we challenged everything, stopping to investigate some comments can be useful. For instance, in class, Tim called the South Side of Chicago, a predominantly Black neighborhood, a "bad" area. In an interview, I asked him what he meant. He said, "It's drug-, gang-infested, and it's really poor. . . . Kids are bad there." As he spoke with me more in depth about his statement, however, Tim began to question the accuracy of his characterization of Chicago's South Side as "bad." He realized that maybe not all the kids there were bad and that maybe his analysis was superficial: "Like maybe not all of 'em, but on the surface it's a bad part of town to be in."

- We need to look and listen for the teachable moments when we might investigate essentializing and colorblindness. When he was talking about his anger at Blacks for not understanding him, Tim touched on an institutional issue, employment, ("You can get a job") and referred to issues that could lead to discussion of White privilege ("what it's like to have Black people think that you're against them just cause you're White"). We can use statements like these as openings where we might step in and ask a question or point out a connection. While student-centered conversations are important, interrupting them to question assumptions forces us to interrogate how we read and characterize our social, economic, and political worlds. This is an integral aspect of developing racial literacy.

CHARACTERIZATIONS OF RACISM

Racial literacy requires that we recognize and address a full range of meanings of racism, including how institutions perpetuate racism. In Ann and Lewis's class, people did so sometimes. However, they also characterized racism as a thing of the past, as a thing that consisted of extreme words or actions, and as a personal thing that individuals can change or overcome.

Racism as a Thing of the Past

"I wasn't even born. I wasn't an idea," Leslie asserted forcefully in class. Arguing that she should not be responsible for racist incidents of the past, Leslie avoided looking at the long history of racism in the United States and at how racism continues to be perpetuated today. In an individual interview, she complained, "It's constantly thrown in your face that, oh, a long time ago White people did this to Black people. And, you know what? I don't care, because that was a long time ago and I wasn't part of it."

Leslie justified her resistance to talking about racism that exists today by what educator Mary Poplin (1999) calls "grandfather stories." Poplin explains that referring only to racism in the past is an excuse for not looking at current forms of racism. She argues that such an excuse constitutes the most dangerous way to talk about racism because saying that there is no more racism shuts the conversation down.

Although students did not often explicitly state that they saw racism as a thing of the past during class, they often said this to me outside class. In interviews, two White students told literal grandfather stories. They explained that their grandparents' racism was simply a product of their times. In doing so, they distanced themselves from older generations:

> Tim: [My grandfather] grew up in a whole different time than me. Like, I can't blame him. I can disagree with him, but I can't blame him. He grew up when segregation was around, like serious segregation. Like, he was in his twenties, and stuff, when they had to use separate drinking fountains. So, like, he grew up in a different time. So, I kind of like— [His racist comments] kind of made me uncomfortable but at the same time that's just the way he grew up.

The students discussed historical racism as if it existed in a vacuum, with no connection to their own beliefs. Although their grandfathers' racism made them uncomfortable, their claim of distance allowed them to believe that racism was not something they had to worry about. This was markedly different from the class discussion about the photograph of a man fixing his grandson's KKK robe. In that discussion, students grappled with the idea that racism is passed down from generation to generation.

Flores, in an interview, said, "Back in the days there was just racism." When I asked if it still exists today, he replied, "Hmm. A little bit. Not to the extent that it was." Similarly, after watching a portion of a movie about racial discrimination in the 1950s, Hank said in an interview, "We know how it is back then. What's going through my head is, 'Nowadays I'm not like that.'" Like Leslie, Hank explicitly distinguished himself from the Whites in the past who discriminated.

Thinking they should be colorblind and that racism was a thing of the past, many students got annoyed when Lewis talked about racism. In an interview Leslie stated, "Lewis is obsessed with the past, and all that racist stuff, and you know, yeah, acknowledgment, but get over it. It's done. It's over. Quit whinin'."

Richard explained that he didn't think discrimination existed anymore and hence his disagreement with Lewis:

RICHARD: Now I think it's fine, but I think Lewis doesn't think so.
JB: What do you think he thinks?
RICHARD: I just think he's seen a lot of stuff. You know, he's lived through a part of our history that I think a lot of us regret, about how our ancestors were. And like I think that just molds his whole opinion on how his culture and his race is living now.
JB: How do you think his race is living now?
RICHARD: I think he thinks that they're all trying to live, but society somehow keeps screwin' em. I think that's what he thinks, but— I don't know. I don't think it's like that.

Richard understood that Lewis's experiences shaped his opinions, but he attributed his view to a generational difference.

When I asked them to explain their assertions that racism no longer existed, several students attributed the end of racism to an amorphous evolution. Tim quoted a Black television character who said, "'Well, I guess what I gotta realize is I got it better than my dad did. My dad had it better than his dad did.'" Even Edmund, the student most articulate about the extent of institutionalized racism, told me in one interview that racism was dying out.

I agree with these students in thinking that racism has changed and become less egregious. It has not, however, died out. The racism of the past is the parent to racism today. Students, however, did not have evidence of that relationship, or of the ways in which racism manifests itself in the present.

Racism as Extreme Actions or Words

"I don't blame any of the White people that are alive now," Edmund reassured Leslie when she argued she was not racist. "But I do have beef with the people who are still out there running around with white sheets over their head, you know, burning crosses." In this statement, Edmund characterized racism as an extreme phenomenon.

Psychologist Beverly Tatum (1997) describes the way in which White people often only see blatant aspects of racism, although these constitute only a fraction of the spectrum of racist acts. Edmund is not White, but Tatum's analysis still relates to his comment: "For many White people, the image of a racist is a hood-wearing Klan member or a name-calling Archie Bunker figure. These images represent what might be called *active racism*, blatant, intentional acts of racial bigotry and discrimination" (p. 11).

Other students also voiced this narrow vision of active racism. In the story about his grandfather, Tim implied that if you do not sound racist, you are not racist. The inference that he and others made was that only explicitly racist statements or actions marked someone as a racist. Similarly, in an interview, Hank offered the KKK as the only example of racism:

> JB: If somebody were to make a movie showing racism today, what would they show?
> HANK: Probably the Ku Klux Klan, or somethin', somethin' like that. I don't really know.

In this response, Hank gave only extreme forms of discrimination or hatred as evidence of racism today.

Sometimes students recognized more subtle forms of racism. Hank went on to describe how his boss treated Black customers differently from White customers. Students occasionally mentioned how racist systems privilege Whites: Philip said that the right to buy a gun was "guaranteed if you don't have a record, and you are middle-aged, and you're White." These comments are important to acknowledge and address.

In some ways, students' definitions of racism are simply a question of semantics. However, recognizing only active racism can lead to what

Tatum (1997) calls *passive racism*. As she explains, passive racism "can be seen in the collusion of laughing when a racist joke is told, of letting exclusionary hiring practices go unchallenged, of accepting as appropriate the omissions of people of color from the curriculum, and of avoiding difficult race-related issues" (p. 11). By not acknowledging that White privilege and other forms of discrimination are at work, students and teachers risk falling into this form of racism (King, 1991).

Racism as Personal

Another way to downplay racism is to emphasize the ways in which racism is personal (Bonilla-Silva, 2003). Jake, for instance, argued, "It's settled in me; I'm not racist. I don't care what color anybody is." In an interview, Tim railed against the idea of discrimination by arguing that prejudice was no more than a matter of individual preference:

> [When you] bring up the fact that you're discriminated against and "Well, this person hates me because I'm Black," how do you know that person hates you because you're Black? How do you know that person just don't hate you because they hate you, you know? Like I don't like a lot of Black people, but I don't like a lot of White people. And I don't like a lot of Mexican people. I don't like a lot of people.

Whether freedom from personal prejudice in this culture is even possible, this logic implies that there is no racism beyond individual interactions.

In addition, when confronted with questions about general patterns of discrimination, students sometimes cited exceptions to argue that racism does not exist. In the class discussion about the criminal justice system, Tim seemed to be fighting to deny institutionalized racism when he cried out, "I get followed, too! I get followed, too!" Similarly, students offered the example of Slim Shady, a White singer, to argue that Black musicians were not the target of censorship. In doing so, students ignored the fact that institutional racism exists despite exceptions. Indeed, tokenism is sometimes used to preserve larger racist systems (Greene, 1997).

Racism Within the Myth of Individualism

A corollary to the idea that racism involves only personal prejudice is the idea that anyone can overcome obstacles if he or she works hard enough.

The myth of individualism and independence is powerfully embedded in American culture, as in Horatio Alger's stories of rags to riches. This myth insinuates that individuals completely control their destinies. One can understand adolescents, who are often working to assert control in their own lives, wanting to call attention to individual competence. This ideology, however, underestimates the ways in which whole groups face institutionalized racism in our culture.

The myth of individualism emerged and was contested strikingly in a class discussion of power and politics. Several students contended that power is a matter of individual merit independent of any other systems, while others called attention to barriers of age, class, and gender oppression. "Everybody has power." Tim stated. "You have power to speak, to react." He went on to say that anyone has the power to run for political office. Malik objected, "Not everyone got the money to run!" The debate continued heatedly:

> TIM: You have the power to get the money. . . . If you have the
>   knowledge and the ideas good enough to support you, you'll
>   get financial backers. If your ideas are good enough . . .
> LESLIE: You have to be in the right job . . .
> TIM: That's what you think!
> PHILIP: You just have to be smart enough.
> LESLIE: If I decided to run for president, nobody's gonna care. They'll
>   be like, "No, she's a woman."
> PHILIP: If you were smart enough, you'd know to get— and you'd
>   watch out enough, making the right investments . . .
> TIM: Do you think everybody in politics is born with a silver spoon?

In this conversation, students' positions somewhat paralleled their own class positions. Tim was from an upper-middle-class family, and Philip's family had been middle-class (although they had hit harder times and were now what he called part of the "new poor"), while Malik and Leslie were both from working-class families. In general, however, students from all different class backgrounds expressed the pull-yourself-up-by-your-bootstraps theory of American individualism, ignoring the effects of institutionalized racism. It may have been that the setting of the classroom influenced this dialogue. There was sometimes a way in which the whole-class discourse clung to "all-American" stereotypes of optimistic individualism and patriotism.

HOW CAN WE RESPOND TO CHARACTERIZATIONS OF RACISM?

Throughout, this section has referred to race and racism as if they were fixed ideas built on a solid foundation. However, students and teachers talked about and referred to race and racism in varying ways at various times. The meanings they created or inferred were not rigid. Characterizations of racism can be seen as fluid, changing, and dependent on surroundings. Given this fluidity, how can teachers help expand students' notions? How can they help students explore the pervasive institutional sources of oppression?

- To counter students' perceptions of racism as a thing of the past, we need to talk about current forms of oppression. School curricula often include clear references to slavery but fewer to current forms of oppression (Wills & Mehan, 1996). As teacher Mary Dilg (1999) wrote, "Many students presently have an incomplete, or in some cases, inaccurate, sense of history. Written from the standpoint of the victors in cultural confrontations over the years, it has given an inaccurate reading of the interaction of these groups and short shrift to the histories of specific cultural groups" (p. 16). We need to connect the dots for students, to fill in the gaps. Lewis did this when he asked students whether people still benefit as a result of the systems of privilege that were set up during slavery. Getting students to think about the persisting ramifications of slavery helped turn the conversation to current forms of racism.
- We need to be explicit about language. If students talk as if racism is only extreme or personal, we can broaden these definitions. For example, to counter the assumption that only active racism is racism, teachers could ask, "If you do not actually say the really racist words, does that mean that you are not racist?" We can label and give examples of the ways in which racism is subtle and institutional.
- Students might assume that it is easy for individuals to overcome obstacles such as racism if they define racism as involving only individual prejudice or discrimination. However, if we define racism as encompassing larger institutional forces, students see that barriers are not so easily overcome through individual effort but require collective and institutional change. We need to be careful of biographical materials that portray unsupported individuals achieving success.
- We can notice and explicitly support students' efforts to examine race and racism in sophisticated terms. In the discussion about

power, Ann reinforced Leslie's and Malik's efforts to argue that classism and sexism get in the way of individuals' opportunities. Although the students did not have precise language, Ann was encouraging: "You're kind of on an issue that might be important." Later she exclaimed "Ah-ha!" when they uncovered institutional sources of oppression. Being supportive helps students continue to talk about race and racism.

CONCLUSION

Although students often characterized race and racism in ways that precluded institutionalized oppression, they wanted to talk about the topics. Many students expressed interest in the whole-class and small-group discussions that raised complicated racial issues. Even Jake, whom other students considered racist, sought out Ann to discuss questions about racism.

Cultivating students' racial literacy is an ongoing process. We are going against years of strongly ingrained formal and informal teaching. Confronted with material that described the existence of racism among her classmates, Leslie, for example, was unable or unwilling to integrate the new information. This stubborn denial of racism speaks to the power of students' previous perceptions in shaping their understandings. Schools' attention to race in history does not necessarily enable students to transfer their understanding to current racist practices. We also continually need to slow the conversation down so that students can examine their unexamined assumptions. "What do you mean and how do you know?" are always good questions.

Even when students and teachers did talk about racism as institutional, they did not always address the issue for long. Within the constantly shifting social dynamics of the classroom, it takes determination to maintain students' focus on loaded topics like race and racism. Students sometimes danced around the difficult subjects by backtracking, contradicting themselves, or belittling their own points. They also sometimes covered up or trivialized the issue by making jokes or changing the subject. Chapter 6 examines the social dynamics in the classroom and posits ways in which we might respond to them.

6

Social Dynamics in the Classroom

As I sat in on Lewis and Ann's class, I was reminded how complicated it is to develop students'—and our own—racial literacy. In several conversations, it seemed as if students would get distracted or only superficially address questions of race. I occasionally felt let down by students' apparent digressions and reticence. I wondered how we might better utilize what students said and did in the conversations.

What did the students bring to the classroom? They brought particular concerns about their social positions. They often wanted to look good in front their peers, see the world in a positive light, and not offend others. They also often assumed that race would determine people's responses to them if they were to talk.

How might the teachers have understood and addressed the social dynamics in this class? How might they open doors that seem closed? In this chapter, I examine those moments when conversations sputtered or halted. Just as Anna Deveare Smith (1993) is interested in the moments when "the smooth-sounding words fail us" (p. xii), I am interested in what happens in those moments when the class seemed to be hitting a wall, sliding backwards, or avoiding the road altogether. These moments can be awkward or tense. What is going on?

To answer these questions, I analyze students' backpedaling, diversions, avoidance of race and racism, and lack of vocabulary to address these issues, as well as the teachers' approach and agenda. Although this chapter focuses on the seeming difficulties the class faced, I do not wish to disparage the actions of the students or teachers. Ann and Lewis were wonderfully skilled, thoughtful, and caring teachers. They juggled numerous curricular considerations. This balancing act caused them to make pedagogical and management decisions about pace, coverage, and fairness that sometimes inadvertently simplified or cut off discussions of race and racism. Similarly, the students in the class were articulate, lively and interesting. Sometimes they were rowdy; sometimes they were graceful; and, for all sorts of reasons, sometimes they avoided the topics of race and racism.

BACKPEDALING

In one discussion, Edmund argued passionately for the existence of racism: "It's always there!" Then, as soon as Leslie spoke to the contrary, he abandoned his argument, readily agreeing with Leslie that racism was a thing of the past. This is an example of the way students retracted, negated, or belittled what they had said earlier about racism.

Later in the discussion, Leslie seemed to recognize something about how racism is constructed: "Partially maybe that could be because we're taught it, even though we're taught that it's wrong." She quickly backpedaled, however. She, Tim, and Edmund abruptly moved away from looking at how people learn stereotypes to arguing that stereotypes "a lot of times could be true, too." Leslie also backpedaled in interview conversations I had with her about racism. She would allow herself to question her perceptions and stereotypes but only to a certain extent, as if questioning the stereotypes she had always believed was uncomfortable for her.

In another discussion, students first said that Blacks and women were more likely to get discriminated against than White men were. Later, they contradicted themselves, claiming that "anybody can get discriminated against at any time." "There's no limit," Tricia stated.

No one likes to be ostracized, and adolescents in particular are interested in maintaining status in their peer group. Lewis said of Edmund, for instance: "Edmund wants to maintain a balance. He sees himself as a leader; and in order to appease people [he figures], 'I can't be an extremist. I have to get them on my side, or keep them on my side.'" Lewis and Ann interpreted Edmund's backpedaling in particular as related to the racial dynamics of the class. They described Edmund as wanting to please White people and posited that he may have backpedaled or only argued up to a certain point because he did not want to alienate anyone in the room. "He's proud of his relationship with White students," Lewis said in an interview.

Students may have used backpedaling as a "survival mechanism," as Lewis described it, when they had gone in a little too far or risked too much in the way of looking bad or being alone in an opinion. Backpedaling, however, does not necessarily signal that students have abandoned interest in their arguments. A week after the discussion about police profiling occurred, Edmund mentioned it specifically as one that had been meaningful to him. This is a hint that, as long as we are respectful, we can call students on their contradictions, and demand that we examine issues thoroughly, despite backpedaling.

DIVERSIONS

One of the ways in which students handled their discomfort was by diverting the conversation away from racism, changing the subject or making jokes. In one discussion, Lewis countered the contention that there was "no limit" to discrimination by bringing up the gay rights ordinance that the class had discussed the previous term. Rather than engaging his point, several students changed the subject and started talking about a boy who had been in the class the term before. Homophobia, like racism, is a topic that can make students uncomfortable.

Similarly, in response to Tim talking about getting "yelled at [and] cursed at" by Black people in a McDonald's, Edmund flatly stated, "Some people just want to be ignorant." Rather than talking critically about stereotypes, Edmund stated decisively, "There's Black people like that and there's White people like that and that's just how the world is. You know?" Although not a diversion per se, his statement pushed the conversation away from an exploration of stereotypes. It makes sense that students want to distance themselves from negative stereotypes so that their peers will not see them in a negative light. Diverting the conversation implies that *they* would not think or do something racist or something that fulfills a racist stereotype.

Another diversion was humor. The use of humor sometimes created a sort of peer pressure to keep the discussion light. Humor is a complicated social act since it can help participants feel connected to a conversation and each other and thus facilitate interactions. Students used "clowning," as they called it, to have fun or lighten a tense situation, but it also could divert conversations from uncomfortable topics such as racism.

Sleeter (1993) conjectures that "a structural analysis [of racism] assumes that how White people view race rests on their vested interest in justifying their power and privileges" (p. 158). One way to explain humor is as an effort to defend a position of privilege. Jake, who often joked in discussions about race, came from a middle-class White family who lived in a predominantly White neighborhood.

Another student who joked a great deal was Vic. Lewis and Ann attributed Vic's self-deprecating racial humor to the fact that he was one of the few Asian students in the school and as such felt the need to act in certain ways to fit in with his peers. Ann explained: "I guess maybe one of the ways he was one of the group was by putting himself down."

It often struck me how much more serious and focused students' conversations about race were when I interviewed them individually or in small groups than they were in the whole-class discussion. Indeed, Ann had bemoaned the fact that the physical setup of the class favored large-group discussion, unlike the previous term, when the class was in a room where students sat at several hexagonal tables and the teachers had used more small-group activities. One way to minimize diversions is to vary the size of the discussion.

RUSHING AND SIMPLIFYING

The pace of the class was quick, and there were several times when topics were simplified. Frequently, in the dynamic exchanges, students and teachers did not have much chance to follow through with important questions or ideas. While the free-flowing structure enabled lively discussion, the class sometimes ignored or lost track of subtle points about race and racism. The following sections explore what happened when the pace of the class was quick, when teachers and students simplified topics, and when the teachers tried to enable students to come to their own conclusions as well as when teachers stepped in to monitor interactions.

Pace of the Class

In one discussion, Ann and Lewis tried to get students to examine the racial nature of U.S. military decisions. In an interview afterwards, Edmund explained his understanding of this as a racial issue. When I asked him why he did not bring the point up in class, he said he had been going to but the discussion was going too fast:

> I just let it go 'cause we kept movin', jumpin' around. So I was just, like, forget it. . . . We were moving too fast and everybody was coming up with different things so quick that it just slid right past it. That's the only reason, 'cause, I was about to say something about it a few times, and Ann kept jumping to other things. And I thought of something else I wanted to say.

The pace of discussion, then, sometimes inhibited participation.

It is important to note that while the pace of class conversations may have impeded more in-depth analysis, the same structure was valuable in getting students involved in the lessons. There was a great deal of freedom for students to pursue their interests and questions in discussions. In addition, students' contributions were often longer than just a word or sentence. These turns were not necessarily in response to a teacher question—a noticeable contrast to the usual inquiry-response-evaluation pattern that occurs in most classrooms (Cazden, 2001). It is impossible to investigate every comment, and teachers doing so might hinder the feeling of ownership students have for the content of the discussion. Ann and Lewis took a similar approach to McIntyre (1997), who chronicled her strategies to get participants to engage in discussions:

> The use of intercommunicative strategies among the participants—laughing, talking, free-associating, participant-led conversations—were [sic] emphasized as tools for extending the discussions about Whiteness and race. My hope was that by shifting the control of the discussions to the participants, they would be better able to "name their worlds" [citation omitted], and in doing so, find those worlds problematic (pp. 36-37).

Simplifying

Teachers have to be sure that students learn certain content, and sometimes the given content seems to preclude deeper exploration of issues. When Lewis asked an open-ended journal question about freedom and allowed students to talk even briefly, he invited conversation about race. There was a tension between Lewis wanting students to talk openly and at the same time—understandably—wanting to be sure students knew that the Constitution is a document that specifies their rights. Students were raising subtle questions about the dispensation of freedom, but the conversation stayed superficial partly because Lewis directed students' attention to the wording of the Constitution rather than pursuing complexities of geography and economics. An in-depth look at the history of the Constitution may have revealed more ambiguous motives and meanings, but nothing more was said.

The class sometimes simplified issues by ignoring the intersections between multiple forms of oppression. One example of glossing over complexities was in a conversation about power. When Ann asked, "How do [politicians] win?" there were several responses: money, class, gender, and intelligence. These are complicated and controversial issues.

Understandably, Ann chose to focus the discussion on one issue: in this case, money.

Making choices and focusing on certain issues happens all the time in conversations and is a necessary part of teaching. We have topics to cover; we have to clarify misconceptions; we must attend to students' attention spans; and we have limited amounts of time. While we might try to attend to complex dynamics of institutional racism so that students can imagine responses and alternatives (West, 1993a), this is a tall order.

Analyzing intersections of race, class, and gender is a sophisticated task. It is unrealistic to expect that all conversations would address multiple oppressions or even talk about race at all. However, there were several times when students discussed socioeconomic status and it would have been appropriate to introduce questions about race. The O. J. Simpson trial, for instance, was a topic loaded with issues of race and class, but in a discussion about it, students and teachers focused primarily on socioeconomic issues.

A teacher at the school observed that students seemed much more comfortable talking about classism than about racism. In the school as a whole, where the majority of students were from poor or working-class families, it may have been that students' commonality around class was less potentially divisive than their racial differences.

Teachers' Approach and Agenda

In dealing with race and racism, Ann and Lewis let the students engage in a process of self-discovery. This often meant that discussions appeared rambling and diffuse. The choice, however, was deliberate. The teachers believed that this approach would promote more in-depth and long-lasting understandings. Ann identified her reticence about calling attention to racism and explained the dilemma of not wanting to impose her views on students. She explained in an interview that she did not think it would work to force a view on students "because it means that I've kind of jumped into the argument, and I'm trying to impose something on them; and that doesn't work. . . . Because I don't believe in hitting somebody over the head with something they're not ready to hear." At the same time, however, the teachers wanted students to think more critically: "It would be good to have them not come back with [so many] knee-jerk responses," Ann mused.

Lewis, too, wanted to promote students' inductive thinking. "If it comes from us," he reasoned in an interview, "it's just another person saying something. But if it's their discovery, it's like, 'Hmm. OK,'" and students would be more likely to understand the point for themselves. After the term was over, he wondered if it might have been more effective to give students some of the terminology and goals more explicitly at the beginning. "We thought about that," he remembered. "Ann said, 'If we tell them this hard-and-fast story, do we have any room to move? It's laid in concrete.' If we tell them this hard-and-fast story," he added, laughing at the metaphor, "then it's dried up already!"

Allowing students a great deal of freedom in discussion undoubtedly led to students' engagement in conversations. Ironically, the teachers' desire for all students to be heard sometimes limited critical discussion. Lewis told me that he wanted students to be polite when they talk and "leave time for other people to talk instead of hogging the floor." Yet sometimes doing so cut conversations short.

As well as monitoring students' turn-taking, the teachers needed to manage the class. When students were shouting rowdily about the terms *Oriental* and *mulatto,* Lewis calmed the discussion down: "Do it after class. Not to squash your wanting to know, but it's like we need to move on." In addition, the teachers stopped students when they seemed to be attacking another student. On one occasion, Lewis seemed to try to protect the White students in the class: "Sometimes I wonder if I was White and if I had been trying to be open and not be accused of those things [racism], how would I feel if every time you see something, you see Blacks being put upon by Whites?"

As humanities professor Michael Eric Dyson (2003) notes of academic talk, statements that reassure some students may simultaneously alienate others: "Discourses of tolerance and civility...strangely enough, are deployed to restrict the powerful expression of more raw, less muted, occasionally rage-filled visions of marginal racial existence" (p. 57). When Lewis was reassuring the White students, for example, he also interrupted a Black students' impassioned statement about racism.

Managing discussions is a balancing act. We need to be sure that students are not hurt emotionally, yet we also need to encourage risk taking. As bell hooks (2003) points out:

> One of the principles we strive to embody is the value of risk, honoring the fact that we may learn and grow in circumstances where we do not feel safe, that the presence of conflict is not necessarily negative but rather its meaning is determined by how we cope with that conflict. Trusting our ability to cope in situations where racialized conflict arises is far more fruitful than insisting on safety as the best or only basis for bonding. (p. 64)

The role of facilitator can compete with the project of critical investigation:

Conversations sometimes got more involved when people did "hog the floor" or got passionate and interrupted each other. Lewis's making sure everyone had a chance to talk undoubtedly was a factor in encouraging student participation in discussion. The fact that this impulse may sometimes have foreshortened conversation does not imply that Lewis's decisions were wrong. Choices such as these are difficult to gauge. "It's always a close call," Ann pondered in an interview. "How long do you let kids [talk]? . . . Sometimes we let them go on too long. Sometimes we cut them off too soon."

Finally, although many topics lent themselves to analysis along racial lines, there were many times when the teachers' agenda appropriately did not include race. In the aftermath of the Columbine shootings in which 13 students were killed in a school in Colorado, for example, the class spent almost a whole class period talking about the incident. Although one can view the shootings, the media coverage of the event, and the public reaction to the event through the lens of race, the teachers did not emphasize this analysis. Teachers and students mentioned racism briefly, but, as Ann and Lewis explained afterwards, their purpose in discussing the event was not to have a lesson in history or sociology, but to help students deal with feelings of grief or fear about what had occurred.

AVOIDANCE

In addition to diverting or simplifying conversations about race or racism, sometimes students avoided them. Because avoidance is not always visible, this aspect of talking about racism is perhaps the most difficult to identify and explain. Why did students shy away from topics that clearly interested them? Sometimes White students did not want to deal with race with a Black teacher. In addition, students wanted to remain positive; they worried about how others would perceive them; and they were influenced by power dynamics and their lack of vocabulary.

Impact of Teachers' Race

When Lewis brought up the topic of race, students often ignored him or changed the subject. In interviews, students voiced anger, confusion, and resentment at the fact that Lewis talked about race as often as he did. Most students liked Lewis, so their ambivalence was striking. At the same time, students did not exhibit or express such resistance to Ann's bringing up the topic of race. Why was there a difference? Did the two teachers raise the topic differently? What was the impact of the fact that Ann is White and Lewis is Black?

In a discussion of rights guaranteed to Americans, students were unusually quiet and attentive when Lewis told a story about segregation, but when he finished they ignored it. When I talked to Richard about this conversation, he dismissed Lewis' story: "Lewis was trying to say, like back in the day, how the slaves and stuff their rights weren't guaranteed at all." One could attribute Richard's misinterpretation to an inaccurate sense of history, but it was also a way to reject the relevance of Lewis' point.

Tim also expressed conflicted reactions to Lewis's conversations about racism. While he did not exactly think racism was a thing of the past, Tim said that if we kept talking about it, it would persist: "How are you going to get past racism if you dwell on it? If you just sit there and write poems about it and bring it up in class and talk about it, how are you going to get past it? You can't dwell on it."

Like Tim, Jake was vehement in his anger at Lewis for bringing up racism so much. Speaking in a group interview, Jake explained: "Every day Lewis brings [racism] up, [or] somebody brings it up, the more I've got to think about it.... I don't understand why we can't just move on."

Students' negative reactions to Lewis were complicated by their clear admiration for him. Tim expressed appreciation for Lewis having talked about race. In an interview in the middle of April, he explained his changing view of Lewis:

> I had thought before [that] Lewis thinks that we—this is what I thought before—Lewis thinks that we have it in for him. We don't like him because of his color. We won't give him an opportunity that we would give somebody else that's White because he's Black. And I was thinking, "Why does he gotta beat it into our heads?!" Like, yeah. I know! I know what happened 400 years ago! I know what happened with the slaves. I know about this. But now I think that being in this class makes me more apt to put myself in his shoes.

Tim appreciated his teacher: "He's just trying to educate us as to what happened, and how to make it a little better."

Similarly, Jake expressed appreciation of Lewis. They often joked together in and out of class. Ann described Jake as liking Lewis a great deal. She put Jake in a category of White students whom Lewis had profoundly influenced:

ANN: There were three or four White guys during the whole time
that I was working with Lewis, that I think were incredibly
influenced by having him as a teacher or as an advisor.

JB: Influenced?

ANN: To be not racist! I mean to examine their racism (*pause*)
because they couldn't like him *and* be racist. And that was
really hard for some of them, but they really liked him.

One of the ways in which Jake and other students may have
reconciled their racist beliefs with the fact that they liked Lewis was by
"de-racing" Lewis, that is, minimizing or ignoring Lewis's Blackness (K.
Sanders, personal communication, Oct. 21, 2000). It makes sense, if that
was the case, that those students would have a strong reaction when
Lewis, through calling attention to race, made it difficult for them to
maintain their contradictory beliefs.

Why didn't students respond so negatively to Ann bringing up race or
racism? Ann and Lewis had different styles. While Ann, who often used
questions to get at a point, did bring up racism, Lewis did so more directly.
In a discussion of the U.S. military involvement in Kosovo, Ann tried to
point out the discrepancy between military policy in predominantly White
Europe and predominantly Black Africa. Ann did not use the words *racist*
or *institutional oppression*. Lewis, on the other hand, talked explicitly about
race. He asked outright, "Could it be that if you're White, you're right?"
In another discussion he asked, "In gang war, who dies? What is the color
of people who die?"

According to Ann, Lewis's directness had intimidated some students
in the past. Ann explained in an interview that, while Lewis was very
influential in shifting some students' perspectives, his direct challenges
bothered other students, even to the extent that they wanted to drop his
class:

There were other kids who couldn't stand Lewis (and a lot of
times they were girls) because he challenged them on— They
would come and complain, "Well I can't stand being in his class
because he challenges me on the racist stuff." They'd leave his
classes.

That Lewis's directness might have had such an impact is a serious
contention. However, it does not fully explain the present students'
reactions to Lewis.

The reason some students pegged Lewis as inappropriately
bringing up race and racism may lie in the fact that Lewis is Black.

Lewis unapologetically referred to himself as Black and talked openly about his race. In talking about how attitudes change, for example, students were silent when Lewis explained that, "As a kid, I thought all Whites were in the KKK." For students who valued colorblindness, such openness might have made them uncomfortable.

Another reason students may have been uncomfortable is that by talking about his race, Lewis broke an unspoken expectation that school is a place where we concentrate on the work of the mind and ignore the presence of the body. bell hooks (2003) points out that academia is a place invested in a mind/body split: "I think that one of the unspoken discomforts surrounding the way a discourse of race and gender, class and sexual practice has disrupted the academy is precisely the challenge to that mind/body split" (pp.135-136). Especially in a school where students are not used to having Black teachers, as Central was, calling attention to the impact of one's Blackness can be problematic.

Another cause, related to essentializing, might be that students saw Lewis as an expert on racial issues, and they therefore do not think they will have anything to add. Cheryl Johnson (1994), a Black professor, describes this combination of effects: "Silence gives [students] some protection from the issues and from me, the authority figure who knows all the righteous answers about race" (p. 416).

Teachers can use their knowledge about how race impacts discussion to figure out how to guide discussion. When students are silent, it may be that instructors need to take the first step in addressing controversy. Johnson (1994) describes her students' relief when she broke the ice to discuss a racial issue:

> I remember trying to engage them in a discussion of why the narrator [in Ralph Ellison's *Invisible Man* reacted so violently to the white man by asking what racist name the man called the narrator. No one said a word. Finally, I uttered the infamous n-word—*nigger*—and I remember not their discomfort but their relief that I, and not one of them, had said the word. (p. 415)

We cannot control how students will respond to our skin color, but no matter what we are, we can use our identity to help students develop racial literacy. The fact that Lewis was Black may have made it difficult for students to engage with him about issues of race, but it also clearly helped some students rethink their own racist beliefs. Jeremy, a White student who had gotten in trouble a few years earlier for writing racist graffiti on a school building, explained how he had changed his attitude about Blacks as a result of knowing Lewis:

I got to respect him [Lewis] as a coach and as a person 'cause he just, like, treated me, like, nice, and good, and stuff. And he gave me opportunity on the football team. . . . He gave me so many opportunities, and I was just, like, I started going, "these people ain't too bad." You know, they ain't really what I was taught that they were.

Similarly, Ann's Whiteness allowed her access to students, and she was then able to help them make sense of racism. Jake approached Ann outside class to ask questions about a White supremacist website. He probably would not have approached Lewis with the same question. Ann was able to engage Jake in extended discussions about his struggle with his beliefs.

Impact of Students' Race and Social Standing

Race was a factor not only in students' reactions to Lewis and Ann but also in interactions among students. In conversations about race and racism, students listened to some students more than they listened to others. Who got listened to? Who was responded to, and in what ways? The answers to these questions depended on race, gender, and the amount of social power of the speaker.

Race determined which people were allowed to use language for which others were chastised. When Jake, a White student, used the word *colored*, students were hushed, their laughter almost nervous. Lewis corrected him. A moment later, Edmund, a Black student, used the same term, without any comment. Both Jake and Edmund were self-assured speakers. The difference in students' reactions was probably based on the difference of race of the speaker. In addition, the fact that students perceived Jake as racist may have compounded their reactions.

Another way that race impacted dialogue was that Black students were called on or turned to when the topic turned to race. Some resented the way their teachers and classmates seemed only to selectively want to listen to them. In a group interview with Black, Asian, mixed, and Chicano students, Edmund talked about being the only colored (his word) kid in a class where he had been expected to know everything and give the report on topics about Blacks. I asked if that happened in Ann and Lewis's class. Antoine said that he wanted students and teachers to listen to him more consistently, "not just on a certain topic. Whenever you want to speak you should be able to."

ANTOINE: If you look around, you see more people looking at you than other people [when the class is talking about race].

EDMUND: Yeah, when you start talking about questions like that [on topics about Blacks], they always expect us to put our two cents in, whatever.

ANTOINE: Lots of time I don't feel like it, when it comes to like that. I just don't add my two cents because—just 'cause. That reason. You want to take something from my point of view *right now*, but then before you wanted to interrupt, and you know, not let me speak, so I'm just, like—

Edmund and Antoine cited a discussion of segregation in the schools as an example of being expected to give their opinions because the topic was racial.

Antoine generally remained quiet in whole-class discussions. When Antoine voiced his unwillingness to respond when specifically asked a question related to race, Edmund admonished him, "Do your thing, man! If I want to speak, I make sure I speak." Philip and Hank were two other students who made salient points or raised provocative questions in several discussions, but they were not loud and did not repeat themselves to secure the class's attention.

Some students who inserted themselves forcefully in discussions garnered negative reactions. Tabitha, who did not have much social clout, drew criticism when she used the words *Oriental* and *mulatto* in class. Several boys contested her words immediately. They responded in part because Tabitha directed the offending labels at specific people (pointing at Vic and Edmund). It was difficult to gauge, however, how much the class's response to Tabitha had to do with gender. Certainly, students' outburst in response to Tabitha's language was markedly different from their silence when Jake and Edmund used the word *colored*. There were several other instances in the class when students mocked or attacked the contributions of girls for reasons not applied to boys who made similar statements. The boys' reaction to Tabitha may have been a way to find or show gender solidarity.

Focusing on the Positive

In some instances, students' silence about racism can be attributed to their adolescent (and human) desire to avoid paying attention to painful aspects of life. As Ann pointed out in an interview, students shied away from looking at negative phenomena. "They don't want to be depressed about things, even though they're really cynical," she said, laughing at the contradiction. When she and Lewis had used a series of curricular materials about prejudice, she explained, students "got really down. . . . Even though they'll tell you how hard their world is, they don't want us to spend too much time on that."

Sometimes students expressed the tendency to see their worlds in a positive light. Arguing against the existence of political corruption during a class discussion, Jake said plainly, "I've got to trust. I trust the system." Similarly, when I asked whether the entertainment industry was racist in its censorship, students were quick to argue that it was not.

Students also sometimes did not want to acknowledge the possibility that their classmates were racist or might do something racist. Hank was appalled at Jake's use of the term *colored*, but later, in an interview, he dismissed his use of the term: "He didn't mean what he said. Like if he— People don't mean what they really say sometimes."

Chris echoed Hank's reticence in another interview when I asked Tim, Richard, and him if there were any people who were racist in the class. I was amazed at how much evidence Tim and Richard gave to show that Jake was racist and that at the same time Chris was averse to labeling him as such. Tim explained that Jake had said that Milosevic was not bad because he was White, and Richard cited a day when Jake had talked about "Aryans and all that"—but they dismissed the label by saying they were not sure what Jake thought, assumed he did not really care, and was just acting like a typical White male teen.

Along with not wanting to call their classmates racist, students did not want others to perceive *them* as racist. When students reacted vehemently to a discussion about sports logos, Ann attributed their reactions to their fears of being implicated in perpetuating racism:

> It's so upsetting for them to discuss [logos]. . . . It's so emotional. Almost anything else you can talk about, but in that one, they start shouting you down immediately. . . . A lot of it is: if you are wearing something like that [with a controversial logo] and all of a sudden it's questioned. (Not all of a sudden, but it's questioned.) You know, it's kind of like, you've been going along with it all the time, and if you agree, then you've been a racist. And you don't want to admit that, for one thing.

It may have been that the discussion of mascots was an example of a generational difference. Racial attitudes are not static. The interpretation of popular iconography depends on factors—such as historical events, social milieu, and upbringing—that change from one generation to the next (C. Lewis, personal communication, Feb. 19, 2000). Still, students' ownership of logos and their intolerance of logos being questioned were striking.

Not Wanting to Offend Others

In addition to wanting to focus on the positive, many students avoided the topic of race because they were concerned that they might offend others. They wanted to avoid disagreement or hostile responses that they thought might ensue if they talked about race. Richard, for instance, said in an interview that he wanted to ask Lewis why he thought there was so much racism currently, but he was scared to do so—and thought others would be, too—because he thought it would be offensive:

> JB: You don't think there's inequality today and [Lewis] does.
> Where do you think that difference of opinion comes from?
> RICHARD: I don't know. I couldn't say. I'd like to ask him. Ask him where he thinks this is all coming from. . . .
> JB: How come that doesn't get asked in class? . . .
> RICHARD: Maybe they think it would offend him, you know, if you ask him why you think that your whole culture and your whole race is being persecuted. It could offend him, but I really don't think so. I wouldn't like to ask him though. I don't know why. It doesn't sound like a question I'd like to ask him. . . . He could be offended [by the question]. But I don't know. I wouldn't ask it for that little factor that he *could* get offended.

Richard rarely spoke out in class without being called on. That he might not ask any questions is not surprising, but asking Lewis to give evidence for the claim that there was inequality might have initiated an engaging discussion.

Sometimes students were willing to talk about race in class despite their reservations. Tim, an often gregarious and argumentative student, was one of the few White students who talked openly about race and racism in class. Still, he worried about offending others. In an interview, he explained: "I had to think before I said that about going into that McDonald's. 'Cause I was like, 'Is anybody gonna be offended?' You know? Then I'm like, 'Really. They're not gonna be.' But on the surface I think everybody thinks like that." Tim's reticence was not intellectual. He knew rationally that he would not offend anyone. Yet he still *felt* tentative:

I know that Edmund does not *not* like me because I'm White. And Edmund doesn't think that I have it in for him 'cause he's Black. I know that! But, like sometimes that's how I walk. . . . I think *everybody* does. I walk through and, like— That's why people be careful what they say around other kinds of people. I do. And everybody does.

Such a visceral, emotional response underscores the depth and complexity of fears about race.

Like Tim, Tricia understood rationally that she should be able to talk about race. She said she wanted to learn about it, but she had feelings of guilt that were hard to overcome. She could not explain her reticence:

I just feel weird just talking about it. Because it almost makes me feel guilty for being White, like when I'm talking about when Whites used to discriminate against colored people, it almost makes me feel guilty. . . . And I know that a lot of them in there prob'ly wouldn't be mad at me for talking about it, wouldn't think that I was racist for that. But that's just a feeling I get. Like, I want to learn about it. I think it's good to know about it. But I just don't like to talk about it, you know? . . . It's like this feeling is kind of uncontrollable.

Those "uncontrollable" feelings of edginess, fear, and guilt paralyzed her. Dispelling these fears is important.

Vocabulary Issues

Students' fears of offending others often coincided with their lack of language to articulate ideas and feelings related to race and racism. They did not explore the meanings of words, and there were links missing between the ways teachers raised issues and what students were saying.

In interviews, several students voiced their hope to engage in conversations about race but expressed reservations because of their lack of appropriate language. Tricia, for example, did not know whether to say *Black* or *colored people*, and her lack of vocabulary made her nervous:

I feel edgy saying, like, "Blacks" cause I feel like that's like a label, and I don't like using it. And "colored people" just cause, like, there's colored people in there. Sometimes, not all the time, when I'm not on the right— when I say "colored people" I feel like they—

> Colored people in the room might think, like, I don't know. I don't know what I feel. I can't put words to it. I feel like an intensity when I say it in front of them. 'Cause I don't like making it an issue. It's not an issue to me, but-

Even as she talked to me, another White person, individually, Tricia had trouble identifying what words to use. A teacher might help students like Tricia by explaining the histories and connotations of words like *Black* and *colored*, as well as sharing how and why people—particularly in the class or community—respond to those words.

At other times, students addressed the topic of race or racism but did not connect their concrete experiences to the more abstract concepts such as the construction of race. In one discussion, the teacher pointed out how "people of different races tend to have really different perspectives," using the example of the discrepancy between the European American and African American rating of a television show. Students responded by talking about their own personal preferences. One way to interpret their actions is to think that the students began talking about television and the shows they liked because it was an easier topic to handle than racial group differences. The students *were* talking about racial differences; however, neither students nor teachers connected these responses to the larger question of group differences. In helping students develop their racial literacy, part of our job is to give them tools to connect concrete particularities to generalizations or abstractions.

WHAT CAN WE DO GIVEN THE SOCIAL DYNAMICS OF THE CLASSROOM?

- To counter students' inclination to avoid race and racism or their tendency to divert the conversation, teachers should vary the size of discussion groups. Students are often willing to engage in serious discussions in carefully structured pairs and small groups. Although status and power relations are often re-created in small groups, peer-led groupings also provide opportunities for students to interrupt patterns of authority and shift the social dynamics (C. Lewis, 2001).
- In using small groups, teachers can also allow students to caucus in groups that share certain characteristics. It can be beneficial to create homogenous groups in which students might feel less constrained by their fears of offending others or by their fears of fitting in.

Smith (1994) argued that we need to move beyond "boundaries of ethnicity" to develop a more complex language with which to talk about race, but she also identified times when homogenous groupings provide important positive results:

> In some cases these boundaries [of ethnicity] provide safer places that allow us to work in atmospheres where we are supported and can support the works of others. . . . In other cases these boundaries have been crucial to the development of identity. (p. xxv)

- When discussions are heated, sometimes it can be useful to pause and have students reflect individually through writing or visual arts. This gives everyone a chance to gather his or her thoughts.
- We need to acknowledge students' need to be positive but at the same time figure out how to push conversation beyond niceties. Teachers can depersonalize debates about racism by focusing on institutional oppression before examining our individual roles in those institutions.
- One way to handle students' desire to distance themselves from racism is to reassure them that we did not choose to grow up in a racist culture. I often tell students that just as people who live in big cities breathe polluted air whether they choose to do so or not, we learn to be racist because racism is in the cultural air we breathe. We learn it from all sorts of sources, even from people who love us.
- It can also help to have students imagine a temporal distance from the questions they are discussing. Students recognize their disagreement with individuals in the past who did not consider particular actions or beliefs racist, sexist, or homophobic. We might ask students what people living a hundred years from now will think of the current question or debate. Students may be able to think more critically about their own environment by imagining a distance in time, recognizing that values are not set in stone.
- In response to avoidance or silence, teachers can model risk taking. We can play devil's advocate to show students that it is OK for them to challenge teachers' and each others' positions. We can articulate the unasked questions.
- When students like Richard do not ask questions out loud, we can ask them to write their responses. For example, Stephen Brookfield and Stephen Preskill (1999) suggest that teachers ask students to write about the moments when someone said or did something in class that was confusing, surprising, or helpful. Teachers then can

refer to the comments without students having to verbalize them directly.

- Another option is to have students interact via the computer. Educational researcher Mary Merryfield (2000) describes how students are sometimes more candid in online conversations about race and racism than they are in person.
- In racial debates, we can investigate apparent contradictions. In the discussion of police profiling, I might point out that the class seemed to be concluding that police harass women less often than they harass men and ask how that jibes with the earlier tentative conclusion that race was a factor in police actions. How do race, class, and gender intersect in this instance?
- In order to help students like Tricia who are unsure what language to use, teachers can teach vocabulary about race and racism. Doing so does not need to take away from an inductive approach to learning. Helping students become comfortable simply saying words related to race and racism can be an end run on students' silence.
- Reactions to racial differences are tough to tackle, particularly when they are not articulated. Sometimes we can address them head-on. I can ask what difference it makes that my students are talking with a White teacher. Do they think we would talk differently if there were any Arab Americans, Whites, and so on in our class?
- It is not always clear when we have missed an opportunity to talk about an important point, but the beauty of teaching is that teachers can revisit a question. Teachable moments are important, but if they slip by, there is nothing wrong with returning to a topic. A teacher can say, for instance, "Remember yesterday when Philip said that you can only buy a gun if you are middle-aged and White"?
- Teachers need to be aware of selective listening. Looking to one student or group of students to represent a race, for instance, is a pernicious practice that can silence students. Teachers can point out when that is happening and do their best to avoid it themselves. I try to notice where my gaze lands when having conversations about race so that in my classes where students of color are in the minority, I do not single out students even with my physical actions.

CONCLUSION

Within the everyday constraints of our classrooms, our work is to meet students wherever they are. Our work is to shape the environment as much as possible so that students can develop new, more sophisticated understandings and ways of relating, so that they can become increasingly racially literate.

The students in Lewis and Ann's class did not seem as if they were consciously trying to resist talking about institutionalized racism. They appeared genuinely interested in seeing their worlds as positive places and their city and their lives as beyond the reach of racism. To some extent, it was because of their good intentions that students often did not let the topic stay on the table for long.

At the same time, while the teachers wanted to raise issues of institutional oppression, there were structural features of the class that could undermine conversations. The fast-paced dialogue was beneficial in some regards but also often came a cost of depth of discussion. Ann and Lewis struggled with all of these issues while attempting to help students develop their racial literacy. The teachers had to facilitate discussions carefully, and each choice had a price as well as an advantage.

Conversations may seem more difficult when they are interracial, but students can learn a lot if they are willing to put up with some initial discomfort. Indeed, cross-racial discussions provide unique opportunities. As Tim explained in an interview, "I think it's cool because not very often do you have such a, um, multiracial classroom. . . . Like all different races sort of bring all different views to the table, so I think that's tight."

There are good reasons why discussions about race and racism were truncated, sporadic, or superficial. This chapter argues that if we understand those reasons, we can better guide discussions. Teachers can make use of whatever students bring to the conversation. If we are willing to slow down our conversations, we can take students' apparent backpedaling or avoidance as an opportunity to examine the subtleties and complications of racial issues. Like surfers reading the water and the wind, teachers can make the most of what the elements offer, understanding that each wave of conversation will be different.

It is encouraging that despite the challenges—and in some cases because of the challenges—students were able to engage in conversations about race and racism. Happily, many of the factors that seemed to hinder discussions were factors that teachers and administrators have power to affect. How can we learn from Ann and Lewis's class so that we might help our own students improve their racial literacy? The next chapter offers several suggestions.

7

Cultivating Racial Literacy in Our Schools

> When I dare to be powerful, to use my strength in the
> service of my vision, then it becomes less and less
> important whether I am afraid.
>
> —Audre Lorde

To teach is to take a leap of faith. We teach students to meet challenging goals. We teach them to strive for high ideals. At the end of the day, however, we cannot know what students will do with what we teach them. We can give students tests, have them write essays, and ask for oral arguments, but we can't predict the future.

For many of us, teaching racial literacy is a double leap of faith. We don't know what will come of our conversations, and we are not even sure where the conversations themselves will go. This uncertainty can be unnerving. Yet the act of students talking with each other about race and racism is a powerful accomplishment. Students communicate with and learn from each other. They attend to personal, institutional, historical, and current aspects of racism. They engage questions of equity and justice. Moreover, they demonstrate these habits of racial literacy in the very contexts in which they are learning the new knowledge, skills, and dispositions.

Teaching racial literacy is complicated. Ann and Lewis had to pay attention to the mix of numerous ingredients: curriculum plans, students' individual academic and social needs, and unpredictable group dynamics. Statements and interactions that seemed to impede conversations about race and racism were often the very same words and interactions that provided opportunities for engagement. It was possible—despite *and* because of the disagreement involved—to help students develop their racial literacy.

However, just as watching a chef prepare a meal does not make us good cooks, studying these two particular teachers and their distinctive mix of students does not automatically enable us to address issues of race and racism in our own settings. Numerous interconnected factors give each conversation a unique character. The size and mix of the class and the culture of the school impact discussions. In addition, at the risk of essentializing, I believe that different students will talk about race and racism in different ways. Second-generation Laotian students in Providence, Rhode Island, bring particular experiences to the table. Their reference points are different from those of Vietnamese immigrants in West Branch, Iowa. And they are different again from their peers in suburban Seattle, Washington, who identify themselves as White and having no ethnicity. While these students have much in common, variables such as geography, race, socioeconomic status, gender, and age, as well as the particular group dynamics of any one class, produce idiosyncratic opportunities and challenges.

While there is no recipe for creating a class that successfully addresses controversial issues, it is possible to help students develop and practice their racial literacy no matter what the setting. As Ann explained in an interview, "I don't think there's any syllabus you can write [to teach about racism]." But, she continued confidently, "you can do whatever you want. By that I mean if your intentions are good." Ann compared her efforts to address issues of race and racism to her response to some teachers wanting to initiate a new reading program: "If you've got a couple of really enthusiastic teachers that think this is going to work, *anything'll work*!' So I think that's what you've got to do. . . . You've got to get people fired up."

Fired up, we can help our students develop their racial literacy. Formally and informally, we can weave questions about race and racism into our content areas. Whether we are in a classroom, hallway, or cafeteria, or even on a school bus or playing field, we can notice and respond to students' questions or comments related to race and racism. Wherever we are, we can help students understand and address interpersonal and institutional racial issues within our classes, schools, and larger communities.

Engaging students in discussions of race and racism can feel like walking up a down escalator. We climb the moving stairs, but we might not see much progress. Sometimes we can speed up and get closer to the top, but a hidden engine works to carry us back down. The forces against us are powerful, both in society and in many of our schools.

Many of us are in educational systems where traditional content coverage is emphasized. Others are in schools and communities where the politics of antiracist education are extraordinarily contentious. Yet, despite the factors we cannot control about ourselves, our students, and our schools, I believe we *can* talk creatively about race and racism.

What skills do we need to employ to meet our unique challenges? How can teachers get support to implement their ideas? The first sections of this chapter deal with preparing for, initiating, and refining conversations about race and racism within individual classrooms. The next address what teachers can do in concert: How can teachers and administrators shape school structures to support students' racial literacy development?

Some of the lessons I put forward here cohere with commonplace suggestions for teaching: Encourage students to talk and share, give them powerful materials, and so on. Other lessons may be departures from familiar practice and may entail taking risks and learning with our students in new ways.

PREPARING FOR CONVERSATIONS

Developing our own and our students' racial literacy is not a linear process. Teachers must prepare for conversations about race and racism, but there is no way to anticipate all the turns that a conversation might take. However, we can improve our readiness. Our preparation begins with our willingness to persist in the process.

Reflect

Preparing to talk about race and racism entails significant and ongoing self-reflection. How do you identify yourself, and what does that identity mean to you? (Cultural norms are often invisible until we begin self-consciously to unpack their meanings.) What are your early memories of difference? Where do you struggle when it comes to prejudice and discrimination? In what ways do you internalize the oppression against groups with whom you identify? Where did your attitudes come from? For many teachers, it can be difficult to face the ways we have learned to be racist (Obidah & Teel, 2001). It can also be painful to realize how racist the world is. Guilt and anger are important markers. They alert us to the need to find new ways to respond to our own racism and internalized oppression so that we can help our students do the same. Our preparation is critical.

Use Outside Resources

The more we can find out about the particular histories of people in our communities and around the world, the better prepared we will be to help students understand race and racism. One of the most powerful sources of information is stories: How do your neighbors, co-workers, and friends experience race? Are there speakers, book readings, or groups in your area dealing with institutionalized racism? Although it is impossible to comprehend all the myriad dynamics of race and racism—particularly since they change all the time—the more we learn, the better we can guide our students.

Students and teachers can also learn about race and racism through a variety of media. I often refer to favorites such as Gloria Anzaldua's (1990) anthology of essays, poems and stories, *Making Face, Making Soul: Haciendo Caras.* Novels such as Richard Powers's (2003) *The Time of Our Singing*—about two brothers with a White, Jewish father and a Black mother, growing up in New York in the 1950s—open new worlds to me. Nonfiction work such as Ronald Takaki's (1993) multicultural history, *A Different Mirror,* and Randall Kennedy's (2002) searching *Nigger: The Strange Career of a Troublesome Word* provide information and raise new questions. There are many fiction and nonfiction children's books and books for young adults that address issues of race and racism. I also find it useful to seek international sources of news and commentary to hear a variety of points of view about world events.

To help students think about issues of race and power, Ann and Lewis sought out materials such as the Teaching Tolerance curricula distributed by the Southern Poverty Law Center (www.tolerance.org). Facing History and Ourselves (www.facing.org), The American Social History Project (www.ashp.cuny.edu), Educators for Social Responsibility (1-800-370-2515), and The National Coalition Building Institute (www.ncbi.org) are among a growing number of organizations that design and provide provocative resources and workshops that address these topics. The Internet is burgeoning with organizations that address issues of race and social justice (see, for example, the Native American Rights Fund at www.narf.org or the Brennan Center for Justice at www.brennancenter.org) and tips for teachers (see, for example, the Derek Bok Center at Harvard: http://bokcenter.fas.harvard.edu/docs/TFTrace.html#moments). In addition, many local councils and groups serve as liaisons to educators. The American-Arab Anti-Discrimination Committee Research Institute (www.adc.org), for example, uses grassroots networks to reach out to schools in many communities. At the same time, there are numerous racist organizations on the Web; investigating these can provide insight into ongoing racial conflicts. In all cases, I look for people and materials that reveal perspectives other than my own or that analyze events, ideas, and questions through lenses of race and power.

Use Your Own Style

Putting the issue of race on the table is not a matter of charisma or color. Every teacher will use his or her own style and tone. Ann and Lewis had distinctly different approaches in the classroom, but both initiated and helped maintain conversations. They joked, cajoled, and chastised. They drew on their particular experiences and areas of expertise. While developing racial literacy is a serious endeavor, Lewis and Ann enlisted humor and talked with students in a relaxed atmosphere.

One does not change one's style or tone when discussing race. If anything, conversations about race and racism demand that we have personal integrity. When we take risks to talk about race and racism, we move into a realm in which we are not necessarily experts. As a result, we have to ask questions and expose our own learning process. We cannot pretend to be something other than what we are, and students appreciate our honesty.

Invite All Students to Participate

Racial literacy is like a foreign language to many of our students. If they cannot practice and try out the new forms of literacy, they will not be able to repeat these skills in other arenas of their lives. Who is talking? Who is not? Do the reactions of teachers or peers silence certain students? Can you vary the class structure so that all students will participate actively?

Talking about race and racism is easier to do in an atmosphere of open participation. Lewis and Ann valued and encouraged student input. They gave students time to think about topics by having everyone write about questions in a journal before discussions started. They called on students by name, listened to them attentively, and frequently allowed student-to-student exchanges.

In some of the most compelling discussions in Ann and Lewis's class, several students would speak at once, and students would have to speak forcefully in order to gain the floor. This rambunctious give-and-take among students may not fit your style or the needs of your students, but, no matter how you orchestrate it, students need be involved in the conversations.

Create a (Relatively) Safe Atmosphere

I do not believe it is possible to create a space where all students feel comfortable all the time. However, we continually need to help students feel trusting and trusted. Ann and Lewis encouraged students to be respectful, taught them how ("You guys are good about asking, 'What do you mean and how do you know?'—but let's be careful before we make generalizations"), and defended students when they were being spoken over ("Let him talk").

It is critical that we pay attention to students' reactions when they confront emotional issues such as race and racism (Espiritu-Halagao, 2003). Because we often have a variety of students in our classes, it can be helpful to have students caucus in homogeneous racial groups to discuss racial issues. Although we do not want to be confined to them, homogeneous groupings can provide supportive atmospheres where students can talk openly about their racism and develop a positive sense of racial identity (Smith, 1994). It is also useful to share with students the assumption that while we are not to blame for the racism in society, we can assume responsibility for working against it.

Get Comfortable with the Incendiary

While we may work to protect students' feeling of safety in the classroom, broaching conversations about race or racism may take our students or us out of our comfort zones. Developing racial literacy involves, as educator Bruce Fehn (personal communication, Feb. 15, 2000) noted, "getting comfortable with the incendiary." Conversations that are nice and polite often do not get to the heart of controversial issues.

According to teacher Mary Dilg (1999), "There are some moments in these conversations that are going to be hurtful no matter what other students or a teacher can do" (p. x). Hurt and defensiveness may be inevitable. Efforts to be considerate can be a double-edged sword. The same conversation that some students see as scary will be just the beginning of a "real" conversation for others. What one student hears as reassuring, another might interpret as an effort to silence dialogue. Lorde (1984) encourages us to communicate despite the potential for trouble: "I have come to believe over and over again that what is most important to me must be spoken, made verbal and shared, even at the risk of having it bruised or misunderstood" (p. 40).

Good teachers take risks, and if students are hurt or misunderstood, we do everything we can to pick up the pieces. We can remember that students often appreciate meaningful exchanges in class even though they might feel uncomfortable at the time. Similarly, students may be shy about participating but still be engaged and gain from the conversations. The goal, then, is to maintain all students' participation despite feelings of discomfort or vulnerability.

Articulate and Support Your Rationale

As with any treatment of a controversial topic, teachers need to be prepared to justify their choices of materials and approaches to discussion. Sometimes it works best to forge ahead and, as the former principal at Central used to say, "ask forgiveness, not permission." In other settings, teachers should inform administrators and parents when planning provocative curricula. In either case, we need to have a well-articulated rationale for our decisions. Teachers might use the arguments presented in Chapter 1 to explain why we decide to talk about race with students. We can bolster our arguments with documents such as local district mission statements, multicultural policy statements, or position statements on multicultural education or civic education made by national organizations such as the National Council for the Social Studies and other national educational associations.

INITIATING CONVERSATIONS

Introduce Race Overtly

Good students use a variety of lenses to analyze what they see and do. Race should be one lens that we teach students to use. Lewis and Ann continually required students to practice using this lens. They also deliberately put issues of race and oppression on the table through readings, assignments and discussion.

Introducing race can be as simple as mentioning race when describing a person, particularly if the person is White, instead of being colorblind. We can also probe curricular materials. What voices or data are missing from our studies? Why do the textbook authors use inset boxes to highlight people of color? What difference does it make that Fitzgerald's (1925) Gatsby is White? Or that Cisneros's (1991) Esperanza is Latina? These metacognitive questions allow students to analyze traditional content while also practicing racial literacy.

Including race and racism in the curriculum can make schooling more relevant and challenging. If the word problems in math class deal only with train travel and coin tosses, students do not learn about the complicated calculations required for real life. Asking students to understand and solve authentic social challenges that relate to race and racism are likely to engage students' interest and, at the same time, demand that they use required content and skills. Students learning about maps or sequencing might estimate the distance and cost of driving between Jackson, Mississippi, and Detroit, Michigan. The problem becomes a lesson in Jim Crow if students are asked to pretend to be African Americans moving north in 1925, navigating safe places to sleep, buy gas, and even go to the bathroom. Similarly, students can learn their probability and statistics by evaluating the realities of affirmative action in college admissions. What is the likelihood that a White student versus a Latino student will get into a certain college? Engaging these questions, students are able to practice traditional skills in an authentic context and at the same time practice racial literacy.

Give and Ask for Concrete and Current Examples

"The first part of getting better," Lewis used to say, "is knowing you're sick." If they don't realize it already, students need to learn that racism is a problem. To connect racism compellingly to students' lives, we can offer and elicit examples of local and current racism and examples of antiracist actions. Thoughtfully chosen, powerful materials provide images, metaphors, statistics, and other common referents. We can ask for specific evidence about what race means in students' lives. We can also direct students to look up concrete facts. What proportion of the Black, Latino, Native American, White, and Asian populations are in prison, for example. How have homeland security laws affected the imprisonment rate of Arab Americans?

When we encourage conversations about topics as broad as race and racism, we cannot know in advance what information we will need. In classrooms with Internet connections, students can look up information in the course of a discussion. Instead of being wedded to everyone doing the same thing at the same time, we can provide opportunities for individual students to do the messy work of research. If we want students to return to important questions and make measured decisions, we need to supplement our conversations with concrete and current information.

Talk About Your Experiences

As teachers, we can share the times when we ourselves noticed or questioned something racial, stood by or contributed to racism, or did something to combat it. We can also help students understand White privilege by describing times when we witnessed a White person get a benefit not shared by others or a person of color meet untoward opposition. Talking about our own experiences allows students to see that we are personally concerned with race and racism. There is a fine line between a confession and a reflection, however. We should model how to talk about experiences thoughtfully so students learn how to learn from experiences.

Talking about our own racism can make us feel vulnerable. Modeling our vulnerability can help students expose theirs. Having these conversations can drastically change relationships among teachers and students. Teachers remain in charge and lead the process, but they treat everyone as learners. Students almost invariably appreciate teachers' sincere curiosity.

Help Students Develop and Use Vocabulary

How is racism institutionalized? What is White privilege? Why do people use the term *people of color*? Lewis and Ann debated whether to teach such vocabulary explicitly but decided against doing so. When the term ended, however, both wondered if teaching terms overtly might have been useful. Should we at some point establish some shared vocabulary with which to talk about these complex issues? Do students need certain terminology to address issues of oppression?

In general, students are not equipped to discuss many issues of race and racism. Some students overlook White privilege, and many see racism as only existing "back in the day." The social and historical construction of race can be alien, abstruse, and intimidating (T. Davis, personal communication, May 1, 2004). However, we can scaffold these ideas by teaching terms. Doing so allows us to have higher-level discussions with students.

I have begun, sometimes formally and sometimes informally, spelling out terms for students when we touch on the subjects of race and racism (see handout, Appendix C). I have found that having a common language is useful. Distinguishing prejudice from discrimination and individual acts of discrimination from institutionalized oppression can help students see the sources and broader implications of discrimination. Students refer back to the definitions when they are unclear about issues, and I reference them when students are ignoring the implications of institutional oppression.

Once we have taught the vocabulary, we can reinforce the concepts. Students commonly state that they or other people they know are not racist, for example. Arguing over whether a student is racist or not is not a useful challenge. Rather, we can point out that personal racism is not the only kind of racism that matters or that involves us. When we get students to think about the ways in which social institutions perpetuate racism, we refocus the conversation.

Use What Students Offer You

Students often give teachers opportunities to engage them in discussions about race and racism, if only we would respond to what they offer us. The desire to help students improve their racial literacy broadens what we notice as teachable moments. Ann, for instance, took Jake seriously when he asked her about White supremacist groups.

Students' comments and questions are often veiled and tentative. We have to train ourselves to see what students say as offers. It is not always easy to view students' words or actions in this way, and there are often times when we choose to ignore what we do see. Teachers perform a balancing act between talking with students about issues and moving on. When we choose to engage students, however, the opportunities to practice racial literacy abound.

PUSHING CONVERSATIONS

Question, Question, Question

Simply asking questions and reflecting on racial positions goes a long way in opening doors to critical conversations. Questions can probe what students know or think and help them dissect the social and historical constructions of race. Teachers can effectively ask about how students arrived at their thinking about any number of topics.

We can challenge students, for example, when they essentialize race or voice colorblind sentiments. "How do you know we are so different?" "How do you know we are all the same?" "If there are lots of exceptions to the rule you are proposing, how do you know the rule is still good?" When students talk about stereotypes, we can ask where the stereotype came from.

"What do you mean?" and "How do you know?" are simple but provocative questions.

In addition to asking students questions, we can also teach students to ask their own questions. We can model the questions, request that students use them, and praise students when they do. In some of my classes, I have posted a door-length piece of newsprint labeled, "Questions Are a Sign of Genius" or "There's No Such Thing as a Stupid Question."

We have be reflective about whom we challenge and why, and whom fellow students challenge. Are we only challenging White students about racism? Are we turning to the students of color in the class to be experts about racism? Are we ignoring the charismatic students when they say something racist but challenging the students with less social power?

Slow the Conversation

Teachers can challenge students in a variety of ways. When a student uses the term *colored*, we might simply say that it is an offensive term and request that students not use it. We can reassure the student: "You might not realize you are offending people." Alternatively, we can chastise the student: "You need to be careful."

Beyond banning a term or telling a student to abandon a line of reasoning, we can slow the conversation and tell students why we think there is a problem. Perhaps more effectively, we can help students investigate what they say. "What does that mean? Where does the phrase come from? Why do you think people are offended by what you are saying?" Finally, we might not *assume* that there is a problem, but rather pose the question, "Wait. Is what you are saying offensive? It sounds like it might be."

We can also help students scrutinize an argument without feeling as if they have to adopt a certain belief. When students have a hard time letting go of a position, we can sometimes accept the position—at least temporarily—in order to help students examine it. "Let's assume for the sake of argument that it is true that affirmative action does hurt White people. What is the evidence for that statement?" This approach allows the flow of conversation to continue and at the same time challenges students' assumptions about race and racism.

Revisit the Issues

Sometimes we have the presence of mind to challenge or respond quickly to a statement—our own or a student's. Often, however, we don't even realize when something is troubling until long after the bell has rung. Because discussions take unpredicted turns, it often requires time and reflection to figure out how to respond (Dilg, 1999). We can always come back to a topic later. If the class participates in online discussions, we can address the question or concern in a posting there.

In my own class one day, I found myself getting impatient with some students' vehement colorblindness. Rather than get more frustrated, I changed the subject. A week later, I incorporated a short reading about colorblindness and introduced it with a reflection about what students had said in the earlier class. Instead of mentioning names, I framed the disagreement in depersonalized terms: "Some people think that we should not pay attention to race." Having distance and new materials with which to approach the topic made the subsequent conversation more productive.

The more we practice talking with students about race and racism, the more quickly we recognize when students are getting stuck in stereotypes, limited definitions, or inaccurate understandings. It also takes practice to catch when we are having similar difficulties. The more tools we acquire, the more ways we will have to move conversations in new directions.

Allow for Complexity

Teachers sometimes want students to see a simpler point before they can go on to a more complicated one. Students, however, are often able and indeed anxious to see complexities in situations. While we need to be sure that students have the basic information they need, we can also take risks to take advantage of our students' curiosity and vision.

In an effort to talk about racism, we sometimes offer examples that ignore or underestimate the ways in which class, gender, age, and other factors impact people's lives. When students raise the point that other factors are involved, we can embrace their observation and talk about the complicated ways in which aspects of identity and forms of oppression overlap.

There are good reasons why we avoid complex or in-depth conversation. Nonetheless, we can allow for complexity at least some of the time. The world is a complicated place and if we are trying to prepare students to deal with the gray areas of issues, we need to be ready for discussions in which we don't know all the answers. Sometimes we don't even know the questions.

Be Attentive to Interpersonal Dynamics

We are constantly performing for one another. Teachers can be savvy about how students position themselves. We can be conscious that what students choose to say depends on how they anticipate or perceive their peers' and teachers' reactions. In addition, rather than hearing students' statements as announcements of fixed beliefs, teachers can understand that students' positions are mobile, influenced by a variety of factors.

In heterogeneous classes, one way for teachers to help students become conscious of the gendered and racial quality of conversational dynamics is to keep track of how often students contribute to discussion and then share these findings with the class. I sometimes ask my students if they would participate differently if the class had a different racial makeup, and why that might be so.

Be Patient

As teachers, we need to lead the process of developing students' racial literacy, but we need to be sure that our students are with us when we do. To begin, we need to find out where students are. We need to accept them and not be judgmental, even if they are backtracking or silent. Students are not likely to have become racially literate on their own. Moreover, because of the power of racism in society, they might not learn quickly. Racial literacy requires new cognitive and emotional antennae that take time to grow. This is a long-term process.

In talking about race and racism, what may seem like maddening diversions are often an aspect of student engagement. If students talk in ways that are racist or focus on individual forms of racism, these conversations are not failures. Indeed, individual students' "resistance" can be fodder for conversation, allowing us to invite reactions and responses (Moore, 1998). The process requires patience and faith that our efforts will pay off, even if we can't see results immediately.

Reflect on What Happens

One way to maintain patience in working with students is to reflect on what happens in the classroom. Teachers can write in journals, conduct teacher research in their own classrooms, and talk with other teachers to gain insight into the ways in which they talk and interact with students. Reflection allows us to build thoughtful environments and learn from our mistakes. We can look at our classes in general terms: In what ways are we rushing? Simplifying issues? What materials seemed to trigger engagement? With what concepts are students struggling? In addition, we can examine specific interactions: What happened when students laughed at Sam's story about his all-White summer camp? Why did I feel uncomfortable when Anika talked about her brother being Asian?

Know Your Audience

How do we know that it is all right to press on with deeper questions? What signals that we might be going too far? Although I would argue that most teachers do not push their students nearly enough around issues of race and racism, there are times not to push. When do you bring up race? When do you back down? Answering these questions requires balancing priorities and being attentive to our particular settings. Lewis and Ann talked about the Columbine shootings, for instance, without mentioning race. They had a different agenda that day—a wise choice. They balanced that choice with having numerous other conversations about race. Some students reacted negatively to the way in which the teachers challenged them in those conversations. We must remember, however, that the students who are arguing the loudest are sometimes the ones who are learning the most.

In a school with overt racial tensions, teachers might feel the need to address issues more circumspectly than in a school that has already done a lot of work on issues of social justice. Rather than simply proceeding more slowly, however, teachers can get additional help. They might involve parents in decisions about curriculum, for example. The next section discusses ways in which the whole school can be involved in moving students toward racial literacy.

ADDRESSING RACIAL LITERACY SCHOOLWIDE

As individual teachers, we can help our students in many ways. Working in concert with others, however, allows us to multiply our capacities. Teachers can get information, help, and support from other teachers. In addition, we can solicit the support and cooperation of other school personnel, as well as students' families and other members of our local communities. Administrators are particularly positioned to facilitate a school culture that encourages the practice of racial literacy. They can initiate and promote schoolwide conversations about race and racism.

They can actively encourage all members of the community to explore and question issues in a context of professionalism and support. Administrators can also attend to policy issues related to teacher autonomy and student assessment.

Develop the School Culture

Central High School, where Ann and Lewis taught, sponsored a Blues and Barbeque event and usually brought in a speaker or theater group during February to celebrate Black History Month. These events and others like them are instrumental in producing a school culture that values diversity. However, like many schools, there was no formal or explicit commitment to dealing with racial issues. Special events alone do not do enough to help to make students or teachers more racially literate, particularly when they happen sporadically and when little attention is paid to the larger institutional implications of race in the school or society.

Ann described ways in which schools can work to structure and cultivate a schoolwide interest in addressing important issues. While acknowledging the difficulty, she voiced hope:

> I think it goes back to a school making a commitment to include a challenge, or investigation of racism, any kind of gender inequity, anything like that. And then just constantly bringing articles for people to read—and you know how hard that is—having discussion groups, having something built in [during staff meetings], or after school. . . . To make it something that you're gonna do schoolwide, it has to be something that everybody says, "We're gonna work on this." It's not gonna be a unit here or a month of February or something like that. It's gonna be: Whenever it comes up, we're gonna stop and we're gonna talk about it, or look at it or examine it somehow.

To demonstrate such commitment, schools can establish avenues for exploring issues of race consistently. School improvement committees might analyze the racial climate in the school and plan a series of events explicitly linked to an antiracist agenda. The school can co-sponsor these initiatives with local, national, and international organizations interested in improving race relations, such as a local branch of the NAACP or the Anti-Defamation League. Even having a broad selection of publications in the school library or a bulletin board designated for information and celebration of racial diversity are signs, albeit only initial ones, of a school's attention to improving students' racial literacy.

Create Networks

Just as individual teachers can research and reflect on their own classes, pairs and groups of teachers can help each other creatively foster racial literacy. We benefit from talking to one another about our fears, hopes, success stories, and dilemmas. Study groups, critical friends, teacher research teams, and faculty meetings allow teachers to practice becoming more comfortable with the topics of race and racism. Administrators can support these efforts by providing time, space, and resources.

Study groups in which teachers read and discuss books, videos, or other material about race and racism might happen after school or during common prep periods. The California Newsreel documentary *Race—the Power of an Illusion* (Adelman, 2003), along with PBS's (2003) companion online materials, and Paul Kivel's (1996) *Uprooting Racism*, are examples of accessible, provocative material that might provide the basis or opening for conversations.

Critical friends are pairs or groups of teachers who observe in each others' classrooms and debrief their impressions together (Cushman, 1998). Critical friends talk about dilemmas, challenges, and successes without being judgmental. They follow specific protocols to guide their observations and debriefing. Critical friends focus on particular questions (Bambino, 2002). A teacher who wants to introduce race into conversations more often might have a critical friend look for possible openings to use in class discussions.

Like critical friends, teachers in research groups work together to reflect methodically on their own practices and give each other feedback and insight (see examples from the Madison Metropolitan School District at www.madison.k12.wi.us/sod/car/carhomepage.html). A teacher who is concerned that conversations about racism are troubling to students can conduct teacher research specifically to find out students' impressions and reactions. Fellow researchers can then respond to the data collected (Altrichter, Posch, & Somekh, 1993; Burnaford, Fischer, & Hobson, 2001).

Teachers can also talk together in large or small groups in faculty meetings. Meetings are an appropriate place to invite speakers to talk about aspects of racial literacy. Community members can be excellent resources; local experts can provide knowledge about a community's history and social dynamics. Outside scholars or other experts are also useful in that they bring different perspectives and approaches.

It is imperative that those who organize meetings or groups cultivate dialogue broadly and attend to power dynamics within groups. Our commitment to racial literacy is undermined when we have only limited input in discussions, which is a common mistake, according to Michael Eric Dyson (2003): "Not enough structural questions are raised about who participates in the conversation, when and under what conditions such dialogue should take place, and who sets the agenda to determine what's important to know or do" (pp. 55-56). Power is inherently unequal, for instance, among administrators, teachers, paraprofessionals, and janitorial and food service workers, particularly when there are racial differences among the groups. Facilitating dialogue among all staff requires considering these differences and structuring conversations appropriately.

Reform the Structures

Provide flexible resources. On a concrete level, teachers should be free to manipulate their environments in subtle ways. Control over the architecture of the classroom, for example, can help teachers in their efforts to extend critical discussions. In Lewis and Ann's class, the students could all see each other as they sat at tables arranged in a large square. While this is not a prerequisite to fostering racial literacy, such flexibility can allow increased interactions among students. In addition, access to such resources as computers linked to the Internet and a librarian who can point students to information about questions that arise in class helps students and teachers investigate race and racism.

Allow teachers and students to get to know each other well. Students need serious chances to talk with a variety of people. In many schools, tracking leads to de facto separation of students along lines of race and class and thus thwarts the opportunities for interracial conversations, which are invaluable for fostering racial literacy. In addition, because conversations about race and racism can be controversial, it is helpful if teachers and students have relationships that foster dialogue and productive disagreement. Ann and Lewis's school had an advisory system and relatively small classes, so teachers were able to get to know their students well.

Provide flexibility in curriculum and assessment. Teachers need some flexibility in determining their curriculum so that they can address issues of race and racism, both formally and informally. If they are to take advantage of teachable moments, they need to be allowed to depart from scripted plans or from schedules that require relentless coverage of new material.

Teachers also need flexibility in assessment. We tend to value what gets measured and measure what is valued. Teachers and administrators may want to articulate a way to measure racial literacy. Standardized tests that are increasingly tied to school funding do not measure racial literacy. In arguing for alternative teacher assessments, Ladson-Billings (1998) cited cultural competence and sociopolitical consciousness as two aspects of learning that we should measure. While I do not think we should devise any more standardized tests, I do think that administrators and teachers need to demonstrate to students that they value competency in racial literacy.

CONCLUSION

Observing Ann and Lewis's class is like going to the theater. We don't expect to go home and start living like the characters did on stage, but we hope to have been moved by their words and actions. Similarly, reflecting on the issues that Lewis or Ann addressed might influence the way we structure our classes or groups, the way we approach the topics of race and racism, or our attitudes toward students. We will undoubtedly discover and create additional topics and questions.

Many teachers like Lewis and Ann are committed to helping students develop their racial literacy. These teachers imaginatively introduce relevant questions in all kinds of classrooms and communities. Not afraid to learn alongside their students, they know they cannot just teach out of a textbook. They make sure that diverse voices are heard in their classes, and they empower students to deal with the racism in their worlds. These teachers take risks and they change students' lives. Unsung perhaps, struggling sometimes, and often working in isolation, these teachers deserve our recognition.

Talking about race and racism in one or more classrooms will not immediately rid a school of racial tensions or expunge ways in which racism is institutionalized in the school (Banks, 1997; Hargreaves, 2003). Yet even in schools bogged down in institutionalized racism or in communities plagued by racial conflicts, learning and growth can happen through classroom conversations. Talking about race and racism may feel like being in a foreign country, trying to speak a foreign language we have only just begun to learn. Nevertheless, we must try to communicate. Ideally, teachers will have support from administrators. However, even when support is not systemic, it is still possible to broach topics of race and racism and engage students in critical discussions in the classroom.

Teachers can and do bring up issues of race and racism with students, and these conversations have an impact.

In finding new ways of talking together, students and teachers create opportunities and options for responding to our environments and each other. Talk can change students'—and our own—experience of the world. Vic, one of the students in Lewis and Ann's class, described the power of conversation.

"I don't hear any Blacks make fun of Whites, [or] Whites making fun of Blacks [at Central]," Vic told me in an interview, whereas in his neighborhood and at his old school there were racial tensions.

"But you don't hear it here. I wonder why," I asked. "You say it's an edgy subject."

"I guess they actually even talk about it here," he explained. "Like, if you go in [our second-hour class], you might even end up having a discussion about racism, stuff like that. . . . Here it goes deeper, and you go into conversations that might even affect [you]."

Developing racial literacy gives students tools they need to be effective, equitable citizens. As Vic pointed out, discussions of race and racism can deeply affect students, teachers, and whole communities. Indeed, our democracy depends on them.

Research Participants

Name	Role	Self-Identified "Race"	Age	Gender
Ann	Teacher	White	65	F
Lewis	Teacher	Black	49	M
Antoine	Student	Black	17	M
Bill	Student	White	17	M
Brittany	Student	White	17	F
Chris	Student	White	17	M
Cliff	Student	Black and White	18	M
David	Student	White	18	M
Edmund	Student	Black	17	M
Hank	Student	White	17	M
Jake	Student	White	17/18	M
Jeremy	Student	White	17	M
Jim	Student	White	17	M
Leslie	Student	White	16	F
Mandi	Student	White	18	F
Malik	Student	Black	17/18	M
Mike (Flores)	Student	Chicano	17/18	M
MJ	Student	White	15	M
Peter	Student	White	17	M
Philip	Student	White	17	M
Richard	Student	White	19	M
Sammy	Student	White	17	M
Tabitha	Student	White	17/18	F
Tim	Student	White	19	M
Tricia	Student	White	18	F
Vic	Student	Asian/ Korean	18	M
Steve	Visiting Teacher	Mexican and White	42	M

Poem for the Young White Man Who Asked Me How I, an Intelligent, Well-Read Person, Could Believe in the War Between Races

By Lorna Dee Cervantes

In my land there are no distinctions.
The barbed wire politics of oppression
have been torn down long ago. The only reminder
of past battles, lost or won, is a slight
rutting in the fertile fields.

In my land
people write poems about love,
full of nothing but contented childlike syllables.
Everyone reads Russian short stories and weeps.
There are no boundaries.
There is no hunger, no
complicated famine or greed.

I am not a revolutionary.
I don't even like political poems.
Do you think I can believe in a war between races?
I can deny it. I can forget about it
when I'm safe,
living on my own continent of harmony
and home, but I am not
there.

I believe in revolution
because everywhere the crosses are burning,
sharp-shooting goose-steppers round every corner,
there are snipers in the schools . . .
(I know you don't believe this.

You think this is nothing
but faddish exaggeration. But they
are not shooting at you.)

I'm marked by the color of my skin.
The bullets are discrete and designed to kill slowly.
They are aiming at my children.
These are facts.
Let me show you wounds: my stumbling mind, my
"excuse me" tongue, and this
nagging preoccupation
with the feeling of not being good enough.

These bullets bury deeper than logic.
Racism is not intellectual.
I cannot reason these scars away.

Outside my door
there is a real enemy
who hates me.

I am a poet
who yearns to dance on rooftops,
to whisper delicate lines about joy
and the blessings of human understanding.
I try. I go to my land, my tower of words and
bolt the door, but the typewriter doesn't fade out
the sounds of blasting and muffled outrage.
My own days bring me slaps on the face.
Every day I am deluged with reminders
that this is not
my land

and this is my land.

I do not believe in the war between races

but in this country
there is war.

Assumptions and Definitions Handout

INSTRUCTOR'S ASSUMPTIONS

1. Race, gender, ability, etc., are socially and historically constructed.
2. We learned prejudice, often from people who loved us and were trying to protect us.
3. Prejudice is like a smog. We can't help but breathe it in.
4. It is not our fault, but it is our responsibility to work for change.

VOCABULARY

1. *Prejudice.* Judgments we make about others based on a generalization.
2. *Discrimination.* Actions based on prejudice.
3. *Institutionalized oppression.* Systemic and systematic discrimination against members of a group.
4. *Internalized oppression.* Unconsciously held prejudiced beliefs about oneself.
5. *Privilege.* Benefits resulting from being or being perceived as a member of a group.
6. *Ally.* Someone who fights against oppression not directed against him or her personally.
7. *Silencing.* Not allowing someone or a group of people to be heard, be represented, or have power.

References

Adelman, L. (Executive Producer). (2003). *Race—The power of an illusion* [Videos]. San Francisco: California Newsreel.

Almaguer, T. (1994). *Racial fault lines: The historical origins of White supremacy in California*. Berkeley: University of California Press.

Altrichter, H., Posch, P., & Somekh, B. (1993). *Teachers investigate their work: An introduction to the methods of action research*. New York: Routledge.

American Anthropological Association. (1998). *Statement on "race."* Retrieved Oct. 14, 2003, from http://www.aaanet.org/stmts/racepp.htm

Anderson, J. D. (1994). How we learn race through history. In L. Kramer (Ed.), *Learning history in America: Schools, culture and politics* (pp. 87–106). Minneapolis: University of Minnesota Press.

Anzaldua, G. (1990). *Making face, making soul: Haciendo caras: Creative and critical perspectives by feminists of color*. San Francisco: Aunt Lute Foundation Books.

Apple, M. (1975). The hidden curriculum and the nature of conflict. In W. Pinar (Ed.), *Curriculum theorizing: The reconceptualists* (pp. 95–119). Berkeley, CA: McCutchan.

Apple, M. (1997). Consuming the other: Whiteness, education, and cheap French fries. In L. M. Wong (Ed.), *Off White: Readings on race, power, and society* (pp. 120–128). New York: Routledge.

Ayers, W., Hunt, J. A., & Quinn, T. (1998). *Teaching for social justice*. New York: New Press and Teachers College Press.

Bambino, D. (2002). Critical friends. *Educational Leadership, 59*(6), 25–27.

Banks, C. (1996). The intergroup education movement. In J. A. Banks (Ed.), *Multicultural education, transformative knowledge, and action: Historical and contemporary perspectives* (pp. 251–277). New York: Teachers College Press.

Banks, J. A. (1997). *Educating citizens in a multicultural society*. New York: Teachers College Press.

Bartolome, L., & Macedo, D. (1997). Dancing with bigotry: The poisoning of racial and ethnic identities. *Harvard Educational Review, 67*(2), 222–246.

Blumstein, A. (1993). Racial disproportionality of U.S. prison populations revisited. *University of Colorado Law Review. 64*(3), 743–760.

Bonilla-Silva, E. (2003). *Racism without racists: Color-blind racism and the persistence of racial inequality in the United States*. Lanham, MD: Rowman & Littlefield.

Brandt, Y. K. (Producer), Kirkland A. (Executive Producer), Head, H. (Director), &

McGeevy, J. (Writer). (1993). *Simple justice* [Teleplay based on the nonfiction book *Simple Justice* by Richard Kluger]. Alexandria, VA: PBS Video.

Bronner, S. E. (1999). *Ideas in action: Political tradition in the twentieth century.* Lanham, MD: Rowman & Littlefield.

Brookfield, S. D., & Preskill, S. (1999). *Discussion as a way of teaching: Tools and techniques for democratic classrooms.* San Francisco: Jossey-Bass.

Burnaford, G., Fischer, J., & Hobson, D. (2001). *Teachers doing research: The power of action through inquiry* (2nd ed.). Mahwah, NJ: Erlbaum.

Carter, R. T. (1997). White a race? Expressions of White racial identity. In L. M. Wong (Ed.), *Off White: Readings on race, power, and society* (pp. 198–209). New York: Routledge.

Cazden, C. B. (2001). *Classroom discourse: The language of teaching and learning.* Portsmouth, NH: Heinemann.

Cervantes, L. D. (1990). "Poem for the young White man who asked me how I, an intelligent, well-read person, could believe in the war between the races." In G. Anzaldua (Ed.), *Making face, making soul: Hacienda caras: Creative and critical perspectives by feminists of color* (p. 5). San Francisco: Aunt Lute Foundation Books.

Chin, G. J. (2002). Race, the war on drugs, and the collateral consequences of criminal conviction. *Journal of Gender, Race & Justice, 6*(2), 253–278.

Cisneros, S. (1991). *The house on Mango Street.* New York: Vintage.

Cushman, K. (1998). How friends can be critical as schools make essential changes. *Horace, 14*(5). Retrieved Apr. 15, 2004, from http://www.essentialschools. org/cs/resources/view/ces_res/43

Darnton, R. (1985). *The great cat massacre and other episodes in French cultural history.* New York: Vintage.

Davis, F. J. (1991). *Who is Black?: One nation's definition.* University Park: Pennsylvania University Press.

Delpit, L. (1996). *Other people's children: Cultural conflict in the classroom.* New York: New Press

Dilg, M. (1999). *Race and culture in the classroom: Teaching and learning through multicultural education.* New York: Teachers College Press.

Dyson, M. E. (2003). *Open Mike: Reflections on philosophy, race, sex, culture and religion.* New York: Basic Books.

Ellsworth, E. (1989). Why doesn't this feel empowering? Working through the repressive myths of critical pedagogy. *Harvard Educational Review, 59*(3), 297–324.

Erickson, F. (1986). Qualitative methods in research on teaching. In M. C. Wittrock (Ed.), *Handbook of research on teaching* (3rd ed.) (pp. 119–160). New York: Macmillan.

Espiritu-Halagao, P. (2003, November). *Holding up the mirror: The complexity of seeing yourself in history.* Paper presented at the College and University Faculty Association Annual Conference, Chicago.

Federal statutes imposing collateral consequences upon conviction. (n.d.). Retrieved Oct. 5, 2004, from www.usdoj.gov/pardon/collateral_consequences.pdf

Fine, M., & Weis, L. (1993). *Beyond silenced voices: Class, race and gender in United States schools.* Albany: State University of New York Press.

Fine, M., Weis, L., Powell, L. C., & Wong, L. M. (Eds.). (1997). *Off White: Readings on race, power, and society*. New York: Routledge.

Fitzgerald, F. S. (1925). *The great Gatsby*. New York: Grosset & Dunlap.

Frankenberg, R. (1993). *The social construction of Whiteness: White women, race matters*. Minneapolis: University of Minnesota Press.

Fredrickson, G. M. (2002). *Racism: A short history*. Princeton, NJ: Princeton University Press.

Freehling, W. W. (1994). *The reintegration of American history: Slavery and the Civil War*. New York: Oxford University Press.

Gates, H. L., Jr. (1995, October 23). Thirteen ways of looking at a Black man. *New Yorker, 71*, 56–65.

Gee, J. P. (1994). Discourses: Reflections on M. A. K. Halliday's "Toward a language-based theory of learning." *Linguistics and Education, 6*, 33–40.

Genovese, E. D. (1974). *Roll, Jordan, roll: The world the slaves made*. New York: Pantheon.

Giroux, H., & Pena, A N. (1988). Social education in the classroom: The dynamics of the hidden curriculum. In H. Giroux (Ed.), *Teachers as intellectuals* (pp. 21–42). Westport, CT: Bergin & Garvey.

Greene, L. S. (1997). Tokens, role models, and pedagogical politics: Lamentations of an African American female law professor. In A. K. Wing (Ed.), *Critical race feminism: A reader* (pp. 88–95). New York: New York University Press.

Greene, M. (1998). Introduction. In T. Quinn (Ed.), *Teaching for social justice: A democracy and education reader* (pp. xxvii–xlvi). New York: Teachers College Press.

Hargreaves, A. (2003, April). *Social geographies of educational change: The case of sustainable leadership*. Paper presented at the annual meeting of the American Educational Research Association. Chicago.

Hatcher, R., & Troyna, B. (1993). Racialization and children. In W. Crichlow (Ed.), *Race, identity, and representation in education* (pp. 109–125). New York: Routledge.

Helms, J. E. (1990). *Black and white racial identity: Theory, research and practice*. Westport, CT: Greenwood.

Herrnstein, R. J., & Murray, C. (1996). *The bell curve: Intelligence and class structure in American life*. New York: Simon & Schuster.

Hirsch, E. D., Jr. (1987). *Cultural literacy: What every American needs to know*. New York: Random House.

hooks, b. (2003). *Teaching community: A pedagogy of hope*. New York: Routledge.

Ignatiev, N. (1995). *How the Irish became White*. New York: Routledge.

Johnson, C. L. (1994). Participatory rhetoric and the teacher as racial/gendered subject. *College English, 56*(4), 409–419.

Kennedy, R. (2002). *Nigger: The strange career of a troublesome word*. New York: Pantheon.

Kincheloe, J. L., & Steinberg, S. R. (1998). Addressing the crisis of Whiteness. In J. L. Kincheloe et al. (Eds.), *White reign: Deploying Whiteness in America* (pp. 3–30). New York: St. Martin's Press.

King, J. E. (1991). Dysconscious racism: Ideology, identity, and the miseducation of teachers. *Journal of Negro Education, 60*(2), 133–145.

King, M. L. K., Jr. (2001). "Address to the First Montgomery Improvement Association (MIA) Mass Meeting". In K. Shepard (Ed.), *A call to conscience: The landmark speeches of Dr. Martin Luther King Jr.* (pp. 12). New York: Warner. (Original work published 1955)

Kivel, P. (1996). *Uprooting racism: How White people can work for racial justice.* Gabriola Island, British Columbia, Canada: New Society Publishers.

Kozol, J. (1991). *Savage inequalities: Children in America's schools.* New York: HarperPerennial.

Ladson-Billings, G. (1994). *The dreamkeepers : Successful teachers of African American children.* San Francisco: Jossey-Bass.

Ladson-Billings, G. (1995). Toward a theory of culturally relevant pedagogy. *American Educational Research Journal, 32*(3), 465–491.

Ladson-Billings, G. (1997). Crafting a culturally relevant social studies approach. In E. W. Ross (Ed.), *The social studies curriculum: Purposes, problems and possibilities* (pp. 123–135). Albany: State University of New York Press.

Ladson-Billings, G. (1998). Teaching in dangerous times: Culturally relevant approaches to teacher assessment. *Journal of Negro Education, 67*(3), 255–267.

Ladson-Billings, G. (2003, February). *Still playing in the dark: Whiteness in the literary imagination of children's and young adult literature teaching.* Paper presented at the NCTE Assembly for Research Midwinter Conference: Teaching and researching across color lines, Minneapolis, MN.

Leavitt, N. (2002). *The USA Patriot Act: Bad for Jews, bad for immigrants, bad for Americans.* Retrieved Nov. 19, 2003, from http://www.jcua.org/patriotact.pdf

Lepore, J. (1998). *The name of war: King Philip's War and the origins of American identity.* New York: Knopf.

Levstik, L., & Barton, K. C. (2001). *Doing history: Investigating with children in elementary and middle schools* (2nd ed.). Mahwah, NJ: Erlbaum.

Lewis, A. (2001). There is no "race" in the schoolyard: Color-blind ideology in an (almost) all-White school. *American Educational Research Journal, 38*(4), 781–811.

Lewis, C. (2001). *Literacy practices as social acts: Power, status, and cultural norms in the classroom.* Mahwah, NJ: Erlbaum.

Lobman, C. (2003). *"The bugs are coming!": The giving and receiving of offers as a lens for understanding teacher-child interactions.* Unpublished manuscript.

Lorde, A. (1984). *Sister outsider.* Trumansburg, NY: Crossing Press.

Maggio, R. (1997). *Talking about people: A guide to fair and accurate language.* Phoenix, AZ: Oryx Press.

McCarthy, C., & Crichlow, W. (1993). Introduction. In W. Crichlow (Ed.), *Race, identity, and representation in education* (pp. xiii–xxix). New York: Routledge.

McCarthy, C., & Willis, A. I. (1995). The politics of culture: Multicultural education after the content debate. In J. Solis (Ed.), *Beyond comfort zones in multiculturalism: Confronting the politics of privilege* (pp. 67–87). Westport, CT: Bergin & Garvey.

McIntosh, P. (1988). *White privilege and male privilege: A personal account of coming to see correspondences through work in women's studies* (working paper). Wellesley, MA: Wellesley College Center for Research on Women.

McIntyre, A. (1997). *Making meaning of Whiteness: Exploring racial identity with White teachers*. Albany: State University of New York Press.

McIntyre, A. (2003, February). *Making Whiteness a topic of inqiry in teaching and research*. Paper presented at the NCTE Assembly for Research Midwinter Conference: Teaching and Researching Across Color Lines, Minneapolis, MN.

McLaren, P. L. (1997). Unthinking Whiteness, rethinking democracy: Or farewell to the blonde beast; towards a revolutionary multiculturalism. *Educational Foundations, 11*(2), 5–39.

Merriam, S. B. (1988). *Case study research in education*. San Francisco: Jossey-Bass.

Merryfield, M. M. (2000). Using technologies to promote equity and cultural diversity in social studies and global education. *Theory and Research in Social Education, 28*(4), 502–526.

Moore, C. (1998). Re-thinking the story of male resistance in the feminist classroom: How familiar conceptions can keep us from seeing positive effects. *Feminist Teacher, 12*(1), 44–62.

Morrison, T. (1992). *Playing in the dark: Whiteness and the literary imagination*. New York: Vintage.

Nieto, S. (2000). *Affirming diversity: The sociopolitical context of multicultural education*. (3rd ed.) White Plains, NY: Longman.

Obidah, J. E., & Teel, K. M. (2001). *Because of the kids: Facing racial and cultural differences in schools*. New York: Teachers College Press.

Omi, M., & Winant, H. (1986). Racial formations. In P. S. Rothenberg (Ed.), *Race, class, and gender in the United States: An integrated study* (3rd ed., pp. 11–20). New York: St. Martin's Press.

Orfield, G., & Lee, C. (2004). *Brown at 50: King's dream or Plessy's nightmare?* Cambridge, MA: The Civil Rights Project, Harvard University.

Paley, V. G. (1979). *White teacher*. Cambridge, MA: Harvard University Press.

PBS. (2003). *Race—The power of an illusion: The online companion to California Newsreel's 3-part documentary about race in society, science and history*. Retrieved Sept. 2, 2004 from http://www.pbs.org/race/000_General/000_00-Home.htm

Poplin, M. (1999). The global classroom of the 21st century: Lessons from Mother Teresa and imperatives from Columbine. *Educational Horizons, 78*(1), 30–38.

Powers, R. (2003). *The time of our singing*. New York: Picador.

Rains, F. V. (2003). To greet the dawn with open eyes: American Indians, White privilege and the power of residual guilt in the social studies. In G. Ladson-Billings (Ed.), *Critical race theory perspectives on the social studies: The profession, policies, and curriculum* (pp. 199–227). Greenwich, CT: Information Age Publishing.

Reddy, M. (1994). *Crossing the color line: Race, parenting, and culture*. New Brunswick, NJ: Rutgers University Press.

Roark, J. L. (1978). *Masters without slaves: Southern planters in the Civil War and Reconstruction*. New York: Norton.

Roediger, D. (1999). *Wages of Whiteness: Race and the making of the American working class*. London and New York: Verso.

Said, E. W. (1978). *Orientalism*. New York: Vintage.

Schlesinger, A. M. (1992). *The disuniting of America: Reflections of a multicultural society*. New York: Norton.

Sleeter, C. E. (1993). How White teachers construct race. In W. Crichlow (Ed.), *Race, identity and representation in education* (pp. 157–171). New York: Routledge.

Sleeter, C. E., & McLaren, P. L. (1995). *Multicultural education, critical pedagogy, and the politics of difference*. Albany: State University of New York Press.

Smith, A. D. (1993). *Fires in the mirror: Crown Heights, Brooklyn and other identities*. New York: Anchor Books.

Smith, A. D. (1994). *Twilight Los Angeles, 1992: On the road: A search for American character*. New York: Anchor Books.

Smith, R. (1998). Challenging privilege: White male middle-class opposition in the multicultural education terrain. In J. O'Donnell (Ed.), *Speaking the unpleasant: The politics of (non)engagement in the multicultural education terrain* (pp. 197–210). Albany: State University of New York Press.

Spohn, C. C. (2000). Thirty years of sentencing reform: The quest for a racially neutral sentencing process. *Criminal Justice, 3*, 427–501.

Stanley, W. B. (1992). *Social reconstructionism and critical pedagogy in the postmodern era*. Albany: State University of New York Press.

Stefoff, R. (1977). *Finding the lost cities*. New York: Oxford University Press.

Steinberg, T. (2002). *Down to earth: Nature's role in American history*. New York: Oxford University Press.

Strauss, A. L. (1987). *Qualitative analysis for social scientists*. Cambridge, England: Cambridge University Press.

Stuart, G. (2003). *Discriminating risk: The U.S. mortgage lending industry in the twentieth century*. Ithaca, NY: Cornell University Press.

Sugrue, T. J. (1999). Expert report of Thomas J. Sugrue. *Gratz et al. v. Bollinger et al*. Retrieved April 2, 2003, from http://www. umich.edu/~urel/admissions/legal/expert/sugru4.html

Takaki, R. (1993). *A different mirror: A history of multicultural America*. Boston: Little, Brown.

Tatum, B. D. (1992). Talking about race, learning about racism: The application of racial identity development theory in the classroom. *Harvard Educational Review, 62*(1), 1–24.

Tatum, B. D. (1997). *"Why are all the Black kids sitting together in the cafeteria?" and other conversations about race*. New York: Basic Books.

Tobin, J. (2000). *"Good guys don't wear hats": Children's talk about the media*. New York: Teachers College Press.

"The Tonto Syndrome." (1989, May 26). *Scholastic Update*, p. 21.

Travis, J. (2002). Invisible punishment: An instrument of social exclusion. In M. Mauer. & M. Chesney-Lind (Eds), *Invisible punishment: The collateral consequences of mass imprisonment*. New York: New Press.

U. S. Census Bureau. (1998). [Population estimates]. Retrieved Aug. 3, 2000, from http://www.census.gov/population/estimates/metro-city/ma98-05.txt

Vygotsky, L. (1986). *Thought and language* (rev. ed.). Boston: MIT Press.

Wertsch, J. V. (1991). *Voices of the mind: A sociocultural approach to mediated action*. Cambridge, MA: Harvard University Press.

West, C. (1993a). The new cultural politics of difference. In C. McCarthy & W.

Crichlow, (Eds.), *Race, identity, and representation in education* (pp. 11–23). New York: Routledge.

West, C. (1993b). *Race matters*. Boston: Beacon.

Williams, P. J. (1997a). *Seeing a color-blind future: The paradox of race*. New York: Farrar, Straus & Giroux.

Williams, P. J. (1997b). Spare parts, family values, old children, cheap. In A. K. Wing (Ed.), *Critical race feminism* (pp. 151–158). New York: New York University Press.

Willinsky, J. (1998). *Learning to divide the world: Education at empire's end*. Minneapolis: University of Minnesota Press.

Wills, J., & Mehan, H. (1996). Recognizing diversity within a common historical narrative: The challenge to teaching history and social studies. *Multicultural Education*, pp. 4–11.

Wing, A. K. (1997). Brief reflections toward a multiplicative theory and praxis of being. In A. K. Wing (Ed.), *Critical race feminism: A reader* (pp. 27–34). New York: New York University Press.

Yamato, G. (1990). Something about the subject makes it hard to name. In G. Anzaldua (Ed.), *Making face, making soul: Hacienda caras: Creative and critical perspectives by feminists of color* (pp. 20–24). San Francisco: Aunt Lute Foundation Books.

Yancey, G. (2003). *Who is White? Latinos, Asians, and the new black/nonblack divide*. Boulder, CO: Lynne Rienner.

Index

Active racism, 88-89, 91
Adelman, L., 128
Administrators, 127, 128, 129, 130
Almaguer, T., 5
Altrichter, H., 128
American Anthropological Association, 21
American-Arab Anti-Discrimination
Committee Research Institute, 116
American Indian, and terminology, 16
American Social History Project, 116
Anderson, James D., 7, 22, 24, 26, 31
Anti-Defamation League, 127
Anzaldua, Gloria, 32, 116
Apple, M., 32, 34
Assessment, 129-30
Atmosphere, and cultivating racial literacy,
117, 125
Avoidance of race discussions, 1, 2-3, 9-10,
18, 93, 94, 100-109, 110, 112
Ayers, W., 34

Backpedaling, 92, 93, 94-95, 112, 125
Bambino, D., 128
Banks, James, 25, 33, 34, 130
Bartolome, L., 11
Barton, K. C., 26
Baumgarten, Ira, 85
BET (Black Entertainment Television),
49-50
"Black English," 21, 79
Black History Month, 127
Blumstein, A., 31
Bonilla-Silva, E., 9, 24, 89
Brandt, Y. K., 39
Brecht, Bertold, 11
Brennan Center for Justice, 116
Bronner, Stephen, 8
Brookfield, Stephen, 110-11
Brown v. Board of Education of Topeka,
Kansas (1954), 39
Burnaford, G., 128

Byrd, James Jr., 9

Carter, R. T., 15
Cazden, C. B., 34, 97
Censorship, 49-50, 89
Cervantes, Lorna Dee, 42, 80, 134-35. See
also "Poem for the Young
White Man . . ." (Cervantes)
Cervantes, Steve, 42-43
Child abuse, teaching children racism as, 66
Chin, G. J., 31
Chinese Exclusion Act (1882), 31
Churchill, Winston, 2
Cisneros, S., 119
Civil rights, meaning of, 39-42
Class/socioeconomic status
and characterizations of race and
racism, 90, 92
and oppression, 11
and race, 33
and social dynamics of classroom, 98
of students, 104-5
Classroom
avoidance of race discussions in, 93,
94, 100-109, 110
backpedaling in, 92, 93, 94-95
challenging students in, 59-60, 81,
85, 102, 110, 122, 123
creating opportunities to talk about
race and racism in, 58-62
diversions in, 93, 95-96
explicit references to race and racism
in, 62-66
fear of offending in, 47-48, 79-80,
84, 93, 107-8, 110, 118-19
focusing on positive in, 105-7, 110
and impact of students' race and
social standing, 104-5
language/vocabulary in, 25, 51,
59-60, 63, 93, 100, 104, 105,
108-9, 111

145

About the Author

Jane Bolgatz taught high school social studies and language arts for 7 years. She is now an assistant professor at Fordham University's Graduate School of Education in New York City.